T3-AYZ-115

D0117327

BLUENOSE

THE TALE OF A SHIP • HER EXPLOITS AND TRIUMPHS THAT

TOOK HER TO GREATNESS • AND OF THE MEN

WHO PLANNED HER, WHO BUILT AND SAILED HER

...AND OF THOSE WHO LOVED HER ENOUGH

TO BRING HER BACK AGAIN •

BRIAN AND PHIL BACKMAN

BLUENOSE

McCLELLAND AND STEWART

BLUENOSE Ⓒ copyright 1965 by Brian and Phil Backman. ALL RIGHTS RESERVED. No part of this book may be reproduced in any form without permission in writing from the publishers, except by a reviewer who may quote brief passages in a review to be printed in a magazine or newspaper.

Paper Edition, First Printing 1975. Reprinted 1977, 1979

ISBN: *0-7710-1000-1*

The Canadian Publishers
McClelland and Stewart Limited
25 Hollinger Road, Toronto

PRINTED AND BOUND IN CANADA

TO

COLONEL SIDNEY C. OLAND

NOVA SCOTIAN EXTRAORDINARY

BUT FOR WHOM

THE BLUENOSE

WOULD STILL BE

AN IRRETRIEVABLE MEMORY

This ... was BLUENOSE

A superb painting recalls a long-vanished sight ...
two Nova Scotia schooners flying down the wind, bound from the Banks
in mad, glad race for home — BLUENOSE, Atlantic sovereign, to the windward.
Every line of the incomparable hull, the proud, defiant lift of bow and high canvas
calling challenge to friend or foe, unforgettably recorded ...

Reproduced by kind permission of the artist Jack L. Gray
Courtesy of the Maritime Life Assurance Company.

pROLOGUE

THE OLD SHIPWRIGHT had launched more ships than years and the small copies of them he liked to fashion were honest and hardy little vessels. They had a certain unfinished look about them; the hands that adze out the fine symmetry of a topmast do not always manage well the intricacies of model building. He worked in a shed beneath his backyard stairs, and it had a woody smell about it that mellowed with the blast heat from his stove and the pungent taint of pine chip. The fading pin-up calendar nailed above his bench looked a little incongruous, crowded as it was by thread and marlin, clusters of tiny dead-eyes and blocks, awls, hammers, needle-noses and tack boxes, washers, plans, stencils, brushes and the rest of the ship-maker's stock.

Another picture was still to be hung. Framed and kept dusted, it lay propped in front of him, atop paint bottles. It was a color print, showing a clean-hulled schooner, close-hauled and lee rail under, with a grand white bone in her teeth. The name on her prow was unreadable. If the print had a legend, it was covered up by the frame. But you knew her. As well as he.

"Well now . . . there's a lotta folk round here what's got all kinds of foolish notions about what made her fast as she was. I suppose I don't know as maybe some of them is right," he'd say while he scored a tiny, sheered deck.

"But I worked on her, you know, and it was always my thought that it was what the weather done to her ribs. See, we got her ribs up around the fall of the year. Now, the frost commenced just about then, and one morning in partic'lar, it hit her pretty hard. Now, I think it might have set her beams. Set 'em like as no man could ever do. Why you know very well that somethin' made her faster'n any other ship as ever came out of Lunenburg."

Sometimes he'd pick up the picture and lay it near you, saying as how old Biggie Himmelman had given it to him years ago, how he'd always thought it was the best damn picture he ever saw of her. With his awl, he'd point out the curious angle in the grand upsweep of her bowline, and trace the amazing length of her main boom.

And he'd say, "I'll tell you somethin'. It was a cryin' shame they ever let her go. Never should of, you know. It was the stupidest thing that ever happened—though I s'pose she'd of gone by now anyways. It's goin' on twenty-some years."

Twenty years easily shadow the memory of ships, unless they are remembered for great battles or tragedy. But it is the legacy of a big Lunenburg saltbanker named *Bluenose* that her name is not far from the tongue of any sailor in this world.

Shrewdly planned, built and sailed, she lived in glory and died in ignominy. She was prisoner to her fate long before that night they slipped her moorings for the last time in Lunenburg harbour. Yet she left a memory too grand to gather legend, but too little to fill the aching void in the hearts of the town that first had conceived, then adored her.

It is different today in that quiet Atlantic Harbour. It's not like it used to be, when to mention her to Lunenburg folk brought down a heavy sadness. The pride in her name, always there, is happier now—as though relieved. And small wonder. When the gulls and the church bells rouse the town to an autumn Sunday, you can walk to church knowing when you mount the hill, you'll look back to see a pair of rakish topmasts high above the roofs of the wharf houses. And whether or not there's salt in your blood, you'll quicken to the sight.

It is simply not in the nature of ships once lost to come home to harbour. Yet the *Bluenose* has. She has come back to a memory that was always far, far more than the teeth of a Haitian reef could claim.

On a summer's day in 1960, a Canadian Press copy boy was sent to Lunenburg, N. S. to cover an unusual event for the national news service.   There, the Smith and Rhuland shipyard was launching the *Bounty*, a larger-than-original copy of Captain William Bligh's eighteenth century square-rigger of mutiny fame.   Her building, commissioned by Hollywood's Metro-Goldwyn-Mayer, marked the first construction of a period ship from the keel up only for the purpose of playing the title role in a movie sea-epic, "Mutiny on the Bounty."

For a first assignment, this was a thrill, but no sinecure.   Instruction had been given to try and find some new "angle" apart from the publicity of the occasion.   Yet, what had seemed so likely to be difficult proved quite to the contrary.   It was found already made in the day's overtones, as evidenced on all sides by the wistful comment of Lunenburgers: "If only this was the *Bluenose!*"

Brian Backman's press story, generally headed "Lunenburg Launches the Bounty - Says Now Let's Build the Bluenose!" sparked interest in many directions, including his father's.   Lunenburg-born Phil Backman sensed the need for someone to convert what was still only wishful thinking into positive action.   He became author of a campaign that resulted in public meetings and appointment of committees to study feasibility of the idea.   While the proposal moved through disappointment to triumph, the senior Backman worked to bind interested parties together in common purpose.

The appearance of Brian Backman's feature article, "Return of the Bluenose" in the *Atlantic Advocate* added fuel to a fire which by then was burning brightly, and was to result two years later in the Bluenose's replica sliding down the same ways that had birthed the great saltbanker.

In the *Atlantic Advocate* story, here adapted and retitled "Proud Harbour," the legend of the *Bluenose* is brought to light in all its colour.   How a working saltbank schooner inspired the affection of a nation, her bright image in the memory of a town that basked so long in reflected glory, and the indomitable spirit of those who willed her to sail again - all these are told by one for whom, as for his father, the return of the *Bluenose* became an irrepressible urge and avocation.

Jack Brayley,
Atlantic Chief,
The Canadian Press, Halifax

PROUD HARBOUR

THE FAMED SCHOONER *BLUENOSE*, once a crack Canadian racing vessel, has been lost off the coast of Haiti, her owners were notified tonight."

To many Canadians, the crisp, emotionless words of a radio announcer, on a dismal afternoon late in January of 1946, sounded the death knell of an era.

To the historian, it was the last chapter in the age of sail; but to most, the death of the *Bluenose* was like the passing of a revered and beloved statesman. She had returned time and again to her Lunenburg, Nova Scotia, port, carrying pride and honour to a nation resting between the storms of two world wars. The aftermath of the second of these wars had seen her forgotten. Now she had met her end. Her back was broken on a coral reef, and, abandoned, she was left to rot away in waters foreign to her graceful hull.

The announcement was factual—almost laconic—but it chronicled the passing of a queen under the most squalid of circumstances. They had sold her. They had condemned her to plod between the islands of the West Indies, shorn of her masts and the glamour of her billowing sails and weighed down by cargoes of bananas and rum: the ironies of fate.

It was a pity, felt many, that such a graceful ship was gone for ever. But then she was old,

March 26, 1921; the fleet was in and bunting was flying
as residents of the Atlantic fishing port of Lunenburg, N. S.
gathered at Smith and Rhuland shipyard awaiting launching of the schooner BLUENOSE.
Any launching called for festivity, but oldtimers could not remember one
commanding such interest and excitement. Immediately BLUENOSE slipped into the harbor,
she was towed to the outfitting basin. Less than a month later she was ready to sail.

and had played out her part, and her loss was inevitable.

The Halifax *Herald* spoke the lament: "Her passing is a national sorrow; the ignominy of her death, a national shame."

Canada was stung by her conscience and ashamed of her betrayal. However, in 1937, a ten-cent piece had been struck bearing the schooner's likeness, while the *Bluenose* postage stamp of 1929 came to be regarded by many philatelists as "the most beautiful stamp in the world." These two facts afforded at least a partial comfort. The story of the *Bluenose*, however, seemed complete. Woodcutters and artists might still make use of her sweeping lines; builders of model ships would at one time or another paint *Bluenose* on the bow of some fresh, new replica; her story would be told again. Still, the *Bluenose* finally had receded into the lifeless oblivion that is the fate of all brave sagas — or so it was thought.

In one small part of Canada, though, there could be no satisfactory memorial. For, in her home port of Lunenburg, nothing could transcend the dull ache resulting from what seemed little short of an appalling injustice. The *Bluenose* had been born a thoroughbred under the careful direction of skilled shipwrights in the old Atlantic town, and she had been sold to serve as a workhorse. In her home port, at least, she would not be forgotten, even though Lunenburgers had mostly themselves to blame. They had sold her. Now, they mourned their loss.

Fourteen years later, Lunenburg once again became associated with a famous ship. From early May in 1960, the Smith and Rhuland shipyard was the scene of almost round-the-clock activity as a replica of the famed British mutiny ship, *Bounty*, took shape on the slipway. She would be used in a new Hollywood version of the Nordhoff and Hall classic trilogy of the *Bounty* mutineers. Crowds of tourists daily flocked to the yards to see shipwrights bend the steamed planks around the great ribs of a 400-ton copy of Captain William Bligh's full-rigged ship. Finally, on a Saturday late in August, dignitaries, guests, and more than ten thousand spectators jammed every point of vantage to see the *Bounty* launched into the waters of the Atlantic.

On that day, the spirit of a town was caught up in exploding excitement! Stranger slapped stranger on the shoulder and exulted: "Isn't this a day!" Yet, it was not entirely the day of the *Bounty*, for, novel as she was, she basked, at least in part, in reflected glory. Her launching was graced by the unmistakable presence of a proud ghost. Even while yard workers could be heard "wedging-up" the hull and knocking away the supports that would start the *Bounty* on her way, a spontaneous sentiment arose and swept the imagination of the crowd along before it— "It could be the *Bluenose*!"

In 1920, the late owner of the Halifax *Herald* and *Mail*, Senator William H. Dennis, offered a massive cup—the International Fishermen's Trophy—for competition among sailing vessels. They would have to be more than fast, for one stipulation provided that to qualify, a vessel must be a worker, and well able to earn her keep on fishing grounds amid Atlantic gales.

In the first race off Halifax in the same year, the trophy was carried off by a trim United States entry, the *Esperanto*, and the *Delawana* from Lunenburg was defeated. To local fishermen, the idea of a Yankee carrying away the silver cup was a humiliation to their fleet. The cup would have to be "brought home." An association of interested shipowners and others was formed, and a young Halifax marine architect who was already noted for his fast racing yachts was commissioned to create a vessel to be both a racer and a capable worker.

It was not an easy problem to resolve, but William J. Roue eventually produced plans which were accepted by the committee. After a winter of work, the 143-foot schooner was launched from the shipyard of R. W. Smith and G. A. Rhuland. Those present on the morning of her launching on March 26, 1921, as well as those who had seen hull number two hundred rise from her keel block, were impressed by her long, plunging lines. They named her *Bluenose*, and the vessel joined the marine fleets of the world.

She was built almost entirely of Nova Scotia wood, by Nova Scotia craftsmen, and few of them doubted that this product of their skills would do them proud.

Angus Walters would skipper her. Small, quick-tongued, but a commanding figure on the deck of his pitching schooner, he was affectionately noted for his love of hoisting full sail and giving his charge her head. He had made his first fishing trip in 1895 at thirteen years of age aboard his father's schooner. He had served a hard apprenticeship in the fishing and West Indies trade, learning to steer during

Schooner armada riding at anchor in Lunenburg harbour composes perfect picture of tranquillity and safe haven, betraying no hint of tempestuous life faced almost daily by saltbankers and crews.

off-watch hours under his father's tutelage, racing his dory against others for the bait wharf, and developing a will "to be at least as good a sailor as any other man." Sailing the *Gilbert B. Walters* in the first elimination race, he might well have won, had he not lost his topmast in the final leg of the contest.

Bluenose did not disappoint her guardians. In the ensuing races, "she trimmed them all." The list of the vanquished forms an epitaph to the vessel they could not conquer: *Elsie, Henry Ford, Columbia, Gertrude L. Thebaud.* These were the American challengers, three of them designed specifically by the best of marine architects to trim the wiry little skipper. Rival Nova Scotia schooners had tried too—ten of them—but they also were doomed to second place or worse.

The *Bluenose* had made herself undisputed champion of the North Atlantic fishing fleet, and that honour was never to be taken from her.

But the *Bluenose* was more than a racer! Those who knew her testify that within her lithe sheer was a soul embodied, a kind of indefatigable spirit. She was a fine fisherman, for she still holds the record for the largest single catch of fish ever landed in Lunenburg. But, it was as if she knew that after the fish had been unloaded from her holds, she would be groomed and dressed with her topmasts for another race. When the gun sounded, it was as if she suddenly came alive and anxiously awaited the command that would let her leave the arrogant challenger in her wake.

This belief of Lunenburgers in a schooner with a soul was spontaneous, not merely one designed to illuminate a growing legend. Go down to the Lunenburg wharves today, on a Sunday morning, perhaps, while the town rests, and ask the first fisherman you see about the *Bluenose*. He'll light his pipe, look out to sea for a moment, and then with mounting pride tell of the courage of that little vessel.

The days when schooners raced from the Newfoundland Banks to their home ports with fresh-caught fish were fraught with danger. There was ever the threat of trouble and disaster among fishermen on the high seas, and the families that raised children without fathers or brothers were all too many. The disappearance of a schooner with all hands was not uncommon. In any case, many of the ships themselves fell

Tern and fishing schooners
ride at anchor in Lunenburg harbor on a Sunday morning...
a rare moment of rest between fishing trips to Newfoundland's Grand Banks
or freighting trips to the West Indies.

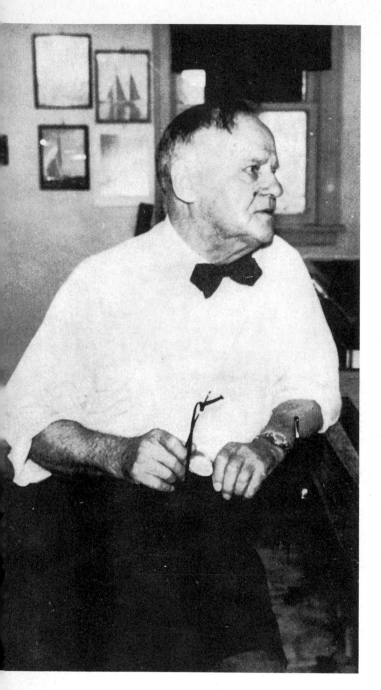

W. J. Roue, Halifax, self-taught marine architect, designed the BLUENOSE.

victim to the toll of the sea. But it was neglect, rather than the sea, which spelled the end of the *Bluenose*. Many times in her career she proved her ability to withstand the worst that wind and wave had to offer.

During Bluenose's maiden voyage as a fisherman, Walters watched a full-rigged ship bear down until his vessel seemed certain to be rammed amidships. The bell was rung, the foghorn sounded, but no action was seen aboard the strange vessel. Walters and his crew finally took to their dories, and, rowing alongside the stranger, spoke to her, shouting for her to "keep off." It seemed certain the *Bluenose* would be cut in two, yet she escaped. Why, or how, is a question that remains unanswered to this day, for the full-rigger did not alter course, and missed the Lunenburg racer by "inches."

The *Bluenose* nearly came to grief again off Sable Island in 1926. Anchored off a lee shore of the Atlantic Graveyard, she was struck by what Angus Walters has described as a "grandfather sea." Her skipper and crew of twenty fought to bring her head up into the gale, but the schooner was swept forward, her cable snapped, fourteen stanchions smashed out, and part of the rail and bulwarks carried away. But even Sable Island could not add *Bluenose* to its list of victims.

"She kept heading up, biting her way into the gale," says Captain Walters, who had taken over the helm for the whole of the six-hour battle. "Don't know as any other vessel could have done it!"

In 1930, she grounded on the rocks of Placentia Bay, Newfoundland. For four days she withstood the battering storms that snarled her rigging and swept her lifeboats overboard, and lived to sail again.

Five years later, *Bluenose* logged a King's admiration, and by the Atlantic's reckoning, her hardest—and perhaps her greatest—triumph. Britain was celebrating the Silver Jubilee of King George V and Queen Mary and *Bluenose* was appointed an official Canadian representative at the event. She made a swift seventeen-day passage from Lunenburg to Plymouth. The port from which Drake once sailed to meet the Spanish Armada greeted the Nova Scotia fishing schooner with warmth and enthusiasm, memorable testament to the acclaim her exploits had earned for her from the island race of seafarers. No less a welcome awaited her from yachtsmen at Cowes on the Isle of Wight, and she was present at Spithead when King George reviewed his fleet for the last time.

The presence of the Lunenburg saltbanker among his battleships did not go unnoticed by the King. Shortly after the review, Angus Walters was summoned to the royal yacht, *Victoria and Albert*. He was received by the King and three of his sons—Prince of Wales, Duke of York and Duke of Kent.

"He was a very nice, ordinary sort of fella," Angus recalled later of the monarch, "though if I may say so, I thought he looked a little frail. Well, we chewed the rag for a while. He had heard some about the *Bluenose*, and he was very interested in knowing about herring fishing. Then the Prince of Wales, Edward, leaned over and explained to him about cod fishing and told him that we didn't fish for herring. Then he told me to come stand by him while they took our picture. He said it was a shame I couldn't come to London and see it on the screen. After we'd chewed off a little more fat, I went back to the *Bluenose*."

The King later sent word that he would come aboard to inspect the schooner, but before the hour of his visit arrived, Angus was told that the King unexpectedly had been called back to London and wished his regrets conveyed to the Lunenburg master.

"I was kind of sorry about that," Angus said. "I didn't carry any liquor aboard the ship that trip, but bein' as how he said he was coming aboard and all, I took him at his word and decided I should offer him a drink. I took him so damned common that I figured he'd be partial to it. So I sent ashore for a bottle of King George whisky."

It was to be expected that his vessel's fame would draw a sporting challenge, so Capt. Walters gamely agreed to a race with several British yachts, including a trim schooner named *Westward*. The course circled the Isle of Wight. There was never any doubt that *Bluenose* was outclassed, for the lovely *Westward* was a born racer, fitted with a giant ballooner and contest sails. She slipped through the Solent and into the Channel just before the tide turned on the *Bluenose*.

"Sure she beat us," said Angus, "but even at that, the *Bluenose* gave her a run for her money."

Her highly successful mission at an end, *Bluenose* shook off her lines at Falmouth and cleared for home. By nightfall of the first day, a gale was blowing. It held with fierce wind

A schooner deckhand at 13,
Angus J. Walters came to sail BLUENOSE to fame.

and seas for the next four days. Laying to under jumbo and stormsail, the ship was leaking thirty strokes to the hour. Angus shortened sail until finally, with his vessel foundering heavily aft, he hove to under bare pole. As *Bluenose* rolled and pitched 150 miles out of Falmouth, one of her ten passengers managed to get the gramaphone working. If the passenger meant the song to provide diversion, the weather witches heard it as a summons; for as the strains of "Anything Goes" filtered up from below decks, the biggest sea Angus Walters had ever seen—a giant, iron-fisted comber —barrelled out of the dark and delivered the fourteen-year-old saltbanker a murderous broadside.

For the first time in her life, *Bluenose* keeled over on her beam ends—her below decks flooded with tons of water. In one blow, the ocean had smashed both boats, the deck-house engine box, the foreboom and the main boom jaws; the galley was uprooted and in shambles, and her port bulwarks had vanished. During the minutes she stayed under, Angus gave up hope she could ever survive. But the mangled champion painfully and slowly righted herself. By now the pounding had opened her seams aft. Angus mustered crew and men passengers and raised flooring planks to shift pig iron ballast forward.

Bluenose's passengers marvelled that even during the height of the hurricane, their masterful captain took time at intervals to come below in high spirits and joke them out of preoccupation with their predicament. Finally the winds abated. Angus brought his wounded charge about and ran for the Channel. He dropped his hook in Plymouth Sound a week after sailing from Falmouth. Except for four hours of the voyage, his mainsail had remained furled. One of his passengers, a veteran of seventeen years' Naval Service, recalled the storm as the most terrifying sea he had ever encountered, and gratefully credited his life to the seamanship of Angus Walters and the incredible qualities of his magnificent saltbanker. Said Angus himself: "I was never prouder of her."

Lunenburgers still remember a sunny morning one September during the Fishermen's Exhibition, at the height of the saltbanker's career, when spectators had packed the wharves for the water sports. Beyond the lighthouse at the harbour entrance were four young schooners, racing on the final leg of a scheduled contest. All at once a fifth schooner hove into view beyond the headlands. It was only an instant

Rare photo shows BLUENOSE on the slip for scrubbing and painting prior to her 1931 series against the Gloucester ship, GERTRUDE L. THEBAUD. Figure standing at left is her master, Capt. Angus Walters.

On the same slip at Lunenburg,
32 years after the photograph facing was taken,
a new BLUENOSE is groomed
for her maiden voyage. Comparing bow views
shows the perfect similarity between
BLUENOSE and her duplicate.

before somebody recognized the familiar silhouette and shouted *"Bluenose!"* and the crowd turned to watch. She was late for the exhibition festivities, returning with her holds full from the Banks. Her topmasts were off, and she lay low in the water. Walters promptly hoisted all possible sail and joined the race to harbour.

Here your Sunday-morning fisherman will say little more, as drawing on his pipe, he'll look again past the now empty harbour, perhaps remembering the way the crowd shouted and cheered that day when the *Bluenose*, heavy-laden, still crossed the finish line minutes ahead of the nearest rival.

Those were good days! In mid-summer of 1933, *Bluenose* stowed her fishing gear and sailed for Lake Michigan as Canada's representative at Chicago's Century of Progress Exposition. For the rest of the season the steps of thousands of admiring visitors sounded homage on the deck of the nautical celebrity. A newspaper story from 1938, following another *Bluenose* victory, tells its own story of the sentiment that was building up around her: "Seafaring folk of Lunenburg will greet the 'Queen of the Seas' when she arrives at her home port," the account reads. "A half-holiday will be declared for school children, while a parade of bands and decorated automobiles, to take Captain Angus and his proud crew through the streets, is being arranged."

But then Canada and the United States became busy with war, and there could be no interest left for the thrills of schooner racing. The submarine battle was at its peak, fishing prospects in the Atlantic were doubtful, and the diesel engine was replacing sail.

Angus Walters had long since opened a dairy business in the town, and the *Bluenose* was less than herself under a substitute master. Besides, she was beginning to slip into debt, for money was still owing on the heavy powerhouse installed within her three years previously. *Bluenose* was owned privately by a group of shareholders in the Bluenose Schooner Company, and her losses were taken personally. Sentiment and interest were hidden by a nation's preoccupation with war. There was but one solution. The *Bluenose* would have to be put up for auction. Then one hour before the Queen of the Fleet was to go on the block, Angus Walters handed over $7,000 from his own pocket to the sheriff.

"I still have faith in the *Bluenose*," he said then, "and I think it is a disgrace that the people

Howard Faulkenham and Dan McIsaac, above, were two of the shipwrights who helped build the BLUENOSE.

of Lunenburg and Nova Scotia would have let her be put on the auction block. I still will protect the *Bluenose* with all I have, for she served me too faithfully to be let down."

But her days were already numbered, and she waited them out, tied to a dock until 1942. The West Indies Trading Company needed fast, light sailers to haul freight between the islands of the Caribbean, and so they made a bid for the vessel.

Little choice was left Walters, who now held the controlling shares. His almost frantic efforts to raise a fund to keep her had been unsucessful, even among his fellow townsmen, who had lost interest in their famous ship's fate. The *Bluenose* would suffer a final indignity. Bereft of her sails, she would die a freighter.

Angus remembers the day she left as a painful one.

"I cast off her lines one overcast day in May. If I may say so, there was a lump in my throat. Somehow, I knew it was good-bye. We'd seen a lot together in fair weather and foul, and the *Bluenose* was like a part of me."

The trim Americans who challenged her, for the most part, had gone too, or else were not to be long in following her. None survived to make the final voyage to the scrapper's wharf. *Mayflower* was burdened with a third mast shortly before she was lost; *Esperanto* was caught by the claws of Sable Island; *Columbia* met her end there too, and she took her crew with her; *Henry Ford* sank off Martin Point, Newfoundland; and the sea claimed *Elsie* off St. Pierre.

The Gloucesterman *Gertrude L. Thebaud* had been the champion's greatest rival. Ironically, she foundered not far from the spot which marks the final resting place of the *Bluenose*.

Yet, memory dies hard, and especially among Lunenburgers! Eighteen years later, a town was still bewildered with grief for the beloved vessel they had condemned. For them, the story of the *Bluenose* seemed to plead for a final instalment. It remained for a totally unexpected event to point the way, and that event was the launching of the *Bounty*.

"Why *not* build another *Bluenose*?" The proposal was an old one, but construction of the *Bounty* cast it in a new light. Here was proof the idea was feasible. They could do better than merely write a worthy epitaph. They could bring her back to where she belonged. Certainly, she wouldn't really be *the Bluenose*, but, in a strangely satisfying way, it would mean having her home again; filling that great vacancy she had left in the harbour, and in their hearts. The imagination of a town was fired!

Mine was too, and so I went to Lunenburg, to the centre of this sudden burst of emotion about a ship, to find some of those who had known her (for many had). I wanted to talk with the craftsmen who built her forty years ago; with the men who sailed and worked her; and I went to Dartmouth, Nova Scotia, too, to talk with the man who had designed the queen.

Bluenose's designer, now eighty-five years old, lives in a large, green frame house not far from Dartmouth's business section. I found him there, working over his drawing-board in a studio at the rear of his home. Perhaps there is some element in the creation of beautiful ships that preserves youth, and if there is, Roue has found it. The famous marine architect seemed, for all purposes, a man half his actual age.

The centre of the little studio is occupied by a great drawing-board, around which are hung on every wall a host of photographs of racing yachts, schooners, and some framed blueprints. The *Bluenose*, strangely enough, holds no place of prominence in this gallery. She is represented only by a varnished hull relief, an old calendar print, and a small photograph. But to Roue, this is not unusual. He loved the *Bluenose*, but he also loved each of the fast, sleek racers whose likenesses grace that room.

The story of Roue is as remarkable as that of the *Bluenose*, for he had no formal training whatever. He began building boats from shingles at the age of five; models of the vessels he had seen from his Halifax window. After leaving high school (curiously enough, over a disagreement with his teacher on pronunciation of a sea term), he was given a volume of what then comprised about all that was known about marine architecture. It was Dixon-Kemp's *Yacht Architecture*, and it was digested in detail by the young would-be designer.

In the hands of veteran sparmakers, spokeshave, drawknife and plane smooth a 90-foot length of Douglas Fir into precise proportions of weight and shape for BLUENOSE II's mainmast.

Smart, sou'east wind teases anchored schooners
as BLUENOSE, in racing trim, beats out of Lunenburg harbor.
Foreground shows busy Smith and Rhuland shipyard
with another schooner a-building on the slip where BLUENOSE was born.

When the *Bluenose* committee commissioned him to design a fast schooner, Roue was not long puzzled. He had drawn the lines for a racing sloop, the *Zetes*, in 1910, which had sailed her way to the head of such sailing competitions of the time as the Wenonah Cup, the Prince of Wales Cup, and the Royal Engineers' Yacht Club Cup. She later went ashore at Greenbank, N. S., in a gale, and there she rotted. But *Zetes* had a greater destiny than being a fast racer, for she was to be the mother of the *Bluenose*. Roue expanded and developed the basic design of the little sloop in the plans which the committee accepted for their challenger.

When I was in Lunenburg, I had talked with Fred Rhuland, who with his brother John took over management of the famous yard from their father. Fred estimated the price of a second *Bluenose* at $200,000. This would include engines, for the ship would have to conform with steamship safety regulations, and must be able to ride out a storm safely if caught with tourists on board.

By the time of my visit, Roue had heard of the idea.

"You know," he said, "I wouldn't be a bit surprised to see them build another *Bluenose*. It was a pity to see the last one go! After all,

visitors still look for the *Bluenose* in Lunenburg. If they want to, they should still be able to see what she was like."

Roue's comment made sense. Captain Spurgeon Geldert, who sailed with Walters on the *Gilbert B. Walters*, is now in charge of the Lunenburg Tourist Information Centre. He had told me earlier that of a grand total of seven thousand Canadian and American tourists visiting Lunenburg last summer, a great many had come expressly to see the *Bluenose*.

"It's surprising how many people don't know she's not here," he said. "They do know that this was her home port, and they want a look at her. They're usually very disappointed, especially when I tell them what happened to her—sold for use as a freighter.

"There's no doubt about it," he said. "Most everybody wanted to see the *Bounty* and were well pleased with her. If the *Bluenose* were here, she'd be a great drawing card."

Roue thought the price quoted by Rhuland was a fair one. The *Bluenose* had cost $35,000 when she was built, and this was high, for the usual cost of a schooner at that time was $25,000. Today's price was, he said, pretty much in proportion to the old one.

"They tried before to copy her," Roue told

me. "They built the *Venture* right from her plans, but they added another mast. She carried a little too much sail."

The R.C.N. training ship *Venture*, renamed the *Alfred and Emily*, later caught fire and sank while carrying a cargo of coal off the Newfoundland coast.

"I bet she'd be good for a tourist attraction," he said, "and to take people out for sails. She'd probably almost support herself, being out every day with twenty-five or thirty people on her."

No one ever really knew for sure just exactly what made the *Bluenose* so fast. There is a wealth of theories, upon any one of which a fisherman will readily expound. Some say that it was from some "unfathomed quirk" in her construction; others say the credit is due to the designer, or to the sailing abilities of Angus Walters. Or, it might have been the sheer of her hull, which, curiously, never left any dead water; perhaps to a last-minute change in her bow, ordered while she was abuilding when Walters decided that the forecastle would be too low. This turned out to be the most prominent distinguishing mark of the vessel—a defined angle which lifted her bowsprit higher, almost to the sky, when she rode a heavy swell.

They could copy the original in design, so that no landlubber or even a sailor could tell the difference, but could they give her that magical speed?

"Another *Bluenose*, right off the plans of the first," Roue commented, "might be as fast, or even faster. There's really no finding out. 'Course . . . the old one was special!"

He sorted through a drawer of heavy blueprints until he came up with those of the *Bluenose*, and we examined them. Shortly afterward, I got ready to leave.

At home on the Lunenburg quays the saltbankers spread their wings to dry.

"I was sorry for Angus when they sold her," he said as we shook hands. "If they do build another, I'd like a chance to sail in her. I bet Angus would too."

I knew there would be little doubt of that.

I drove to Lunenburg the next day to see the man who had known the *Bluenose* best. But first, before I saw the Captain, I walked to the shipyard to discover if any of the shipwrights who had built the *Bluenose* more than forty years ago could still be found working there. I found only three.

It was a busy day in the yard. *Bounty* was tied up at her wharf, looking new and proud with her royal blue hull, and they were preparing to step her mizzenmast.

I asked one of the workers where Dan McIsaac, who was one of *Bluenose's* builders, could be found.

"Anywhere," was the answer, "but if you really want to see him, that's him getting in the car up there."

A minute later I was in the car driving through the town with Dan McIsaac. He was in a hurry, he told me, and unfortunately had little time to talk. But with mention of the *Bluenose*, he relaxed, and after we arrived at the railway wharf, he thought for a minute, and then, looking at me:

"Ah, the *Bluenose*. What a lovely ship she was, and what a pity to see her go. If they're going to build a second though, they'll have to get on with it. Time's limited, and I believe that in ten years it would be impossible to build one like her. There's not many of us older fellows who helped to build her left; just Howard Faulkenham, down at the big shed, and John Rhuland—not Fred's brother—the other one— and myself. But don't misunderstand me. I don't think for a minute that there's any doubt she could be built with the men and carpenters we have. I'd love to work on her before I'm through here."

I found the other John Rhuland in the engine room of the *Bounty*. He sat, cramped between two big engines, smoking his pipe and tugging with a great wrench. I told him what Dan had said about another *Bluenose*.

"Dan's right," he agreed. "I don't think there'd be any problem. And I think there's a good chance they'll build her."

I asked if he would be sorry to see the counterpart of the old racer being used to take tourists for sails on sunny days.

"Nope," he said. "But I'd still like to see her fish, and I'd like to see her race again."

I found others that day who had been concerned with the *Bluenose* when she worked out of Lunenburg harbour; Howard Faulkenham, the third remaining shipwright at the yards who had helped construct her; Willis Rhodenizer. now crippled, who had been cook in her, and who remembers her as "fast as a wild horse."

Little remains of the *Bluenose* herself, but most of what has survived can be seen at the Bluenose Lodge in Lunenburg. Here, bolted to a stand in the lobby, where children can grip it and imagine themselves steering the bucking queen, is the original helm, or steering-wheel. It was removed shortly before she left for the West Indies. Here too can be seen three of the cups won by the *Bluenose*. These precious mementos were given by Angus Walters to Fred Glover, owner of the Lodge. The Maritime Museum in Halifax has her davits. Walters still has a part of her log, and only recently he sent the last remembrance of his famous ship, her bell, to the Maritime Provinces Association of Edmonton, Alberta.

Sentimentally, the return of the *Bluenose* would be a happy event for the town. Exactly how practical, I wondered, would the plan be? Captain Geldert already had told me of tourists' hopes to see her, but I decided to find further confirmation, so I asked Lunenburg's mayor, Dr. R. G. A. Wood.

"I think that for the town it would be a wonderful idea, if it were pursued correctly and with proper promotion. The tourists want to see her, and it's too bad they can't," he said. "I remember the efforts Angus made for her preservation before she was sold. The building of the *Bounty*, though, has brought this idea to a head . . . more than our wildest dreams.

"If they build her, I think it would be a marvellous thing, not only for Lunenburg, but for Nova Scotia, and all of Canada."

There were plenty of suggestions to be heard in the town on financing the idea. Most common was that of a national drive, through contributions of Canadian school children, much like the campaign used to preserve the U.S.S. *Constitution* at Boston, Mass. Each of the students would contribute one ten-cent piece. There were rumours that an association of some kind might finance it. Some favoured a rebirth of the plan Angus Walters began before the *Bluenose* left. It was never executed because it was halted by the war.

(top right) — *Willis Rhodenizer, for a time cook aboard BLUENOSE remembers her as "fast as a wild horse".*

(right) — *John Rhuland, seen here in the engine room of the replica BOUNTY, helped build the BLUENOSE.*

(below) — *BLUENOSE running "wung-out"— poised at sunset to catch every breath · of a soldier's wind.*

After the 1938 races, a citizen's meeting had been held in Lunenburg to try and evolve a plan. They decided to print certificates for sale at a one-dollar price throughout the nation. Each certificate-holder would then be a part-owner of the *Bluenose*. There would be no dividends, except those realized through the increased number of visitors bent on seeing the *Bluenose* and applauding her great record.

After Mayor Wood, there remained only one person to be seen. Hundreds of tourists yearly detour to chat with the 83-year-old Captain Walters. He can be found in a large white house, around the corner from his dairy, where he lives alone with his little dog. He has mellowed some since the day he stood on the deck of his schooner, and scowled and snapped at newsmen whenever he'd heard the Americans were building yet another challenger:

"I don't care for their Mae Wests, Annie Oakleys or Greta Garbos," he had said, "or if they want, Clark Gables. I'll stick to my fisherman's rig."

Now, like his townsmen, the old sailor was enthusiastic about the idea of building a reproduction of the most famous of "fishermen's rigs." Since the publishing of a newspaper editorial and a story on the idea, he had been receiving dozens of encouraging, often highly emotional letters, from across Canada and the United States. One, from Sarnia, Ontario, included a fresh, new dime, taped to a slip of cardboard with the suggestion it be used as the beginning of a national campaign: " . . . as this would be the first dime, I would suggest you bed it in the midship spoke of her steering-wheel. I hope to see the day you will sail a new *Bluenose* out of Lunenburg, as master."

We talked in his living room, furnished with pictures and other mementos of the *Bluenose*. Angus sat stroking the dog which had comfortably settled herself in her master's lap, and commented sadly: "The *Bluenose* was like a lot of men; she couldn't go on for ever. I always expected her career to be remembered, but not with the sentiment felt today."

He would like to see the *Bluenose* race again, in reproduction form.

"Don't know as she'd be as fast as the old one; that's the $64 question, though I really don't see why she shouldn't be if she's rigged and all. Any changes I made in the original, you know, were all above water, and had no effect on her sailing. I think a lot of people thought that change in her fo'c's'le made her faster.

"If they built another, why, she'd pay and repay for herself! If there was something going on up at Halifax or Sydney, we could send her up."

There would be little trouble finding a crew, he thought. It would not take much time to train them—although some would probably be "pretty scared first time aloft."

"They've got a Lunenburg schooner hauled up as a tourist attraction in Cape Breton, at Margaree, I think. But we haven't got one here, in Lunenburg, where there ought to be one.

"I'm afraid that this is the last chance they'll ever have to build another, while interest and feeling is as it is now. There's a different class of people—new generations—and I think she should be built while the fellows are still around who know how she should go."

We continued to talk until it was supper time. Once, the conversation was interrupted by a customer calling to report a missed milk delivery. From where I sat, I could hear the Captain in the hall apologizing and promising he'd send a truck out as soon as possible.

When he returned, I said, "Angus—what *did* make the *Bluenose* the ship she was?"

Captain Angus Walters and the International Fishermen's Trophy.

In dozens of interviews, I had heard the sailing qualities of the old champion attributed in turn to her designer, her builders, her crew, a freak run of luck, and of course, to the Captain himself. Aware the question was more than common, I expected a ready reply. Instead, the aging mariner sat musing in silence for several moments. When finally he spoke, it was to deny himself credit in favour of the hand of nature.

"I think I know what it was. I think it was the way her spars was stepped. If the rest of her is good, a vessel's spars will pretty well tell what she'll do. Somehow, the *Bluenose*'s spars was stepped mathematically perfect, in a way that no man could do. I think that was it. I don't feel as there was a vessel that ever came out of Lunenburg that had her sticks stepped that perfect."

I said good-bye to the Captain and strolled along the wharves. The harbour was bare and empty. Only two steel draggers were tied to their docks, and a small fishing smack was splitting the silence that ruled over the bay. It was getting dark. The sun was beginning to fall behind the golf course across the water, and the little lighthouse at harbour's entrance was only barely discernible.

I realized that I too had become caught up in Lunenburg's almost tearful memory of a ship.

Angus Walters' final words stuck with me: "If they build another, I think I'd like to see how she goes."

I thought of the old sailor sitting there, patting his little dog in the dark of his living room, wondering if he would actually get a chance to stand beside his helmsman, ordering "jib and foresail up!" as the new *Bluenose* cleared harbour; thinking of a day that still might come.

STILL WATER
ASTERN

GROUPED ON BENCH AND BUNK, the schoonermen watched the last bottle strike the deck and rattle to rest among the others already there. Each had an elegant gold label that glittered in the shadowed half-light of the fo'c's'le: CHAMPAGNE

A celebration was foundering. Two dozen Grand Banks fishermen bent on drinking the grandest of events into pickled posterity, instead stared somberly at the glass carnage littering the deck. It was like someone at a toot had poured tea. A bewildered sort of calm had settled upon the gathering, as oppressive as fog and unbroken by a single respectable belch.

It was a growl rumbling from somewhere out of a lower bunk that finally lifted it:

"Vell! Now det ve finished det t'underin' apple chuice, let's bwreak oudt der Wrrum and get down tuh sehwerious drrinkin'!"

And while soft Atlantic harbour swells surged a trim schooner named *Bluenose* taut on her hawsers, the gathering of "all hands" below the fo'c's'le head came nicely 'round, rode easier under a more pungent wind and soon heeled over altogether.

They were skippers all, and crewmen aboard the lithe Lunenburg saltbanker that was to bring glory to a waning era with the fame of her name. That same afternoon—October 24, 1921— the *Bluenose* had romped her way across the finish line a good three miles ahead of the Gloucesterman

Elsie to regain for Canada the cherished International Fishermen's Trophy. The Cup had been surrendered the previous year by Lunenburg's *Delawana* to her fleeter American rival, the *Esperanto*.

It was in homage to her victory that an American admirer, wishing to add to the gaiety and goodwill of the *Bluenose* men, came aboard bearing a gift—a case of "genewine French" champagne, which was received in the spirit intended and promptly finished off with a speed for which Banks fishermen long had been famous.

The crewman's judgment of the stuff—though gruff—was spoken in that compelling tang of Lunenburg dialect, the like of which is not a mark of any place else in the world. Perhaps it was as well that the donor was not on hand to hear his gift labelled "apple chuice." Yet if it sounded like contempt, the derision was gentle. The Lunenburger, himself an expert at hospitality, is not unmindful of a gracious gesture in his direction.

That the delicate French nectar should have lacked something on palates conditioned for years with the stouter rum was understandable. It was also oddly symbolic of the reason for the building of the *Bluenose*, and for the International Schooner Races in general. A fisherman, inured to the incredibly hard life on the Banks, looked to a liquor that could be depended upon to congeal the blood, stoke a belly-fire and warm the gullet in fast order. Anything less—in the nature of wine or champagne—was left to more genteel tastes. To the doryman, rum, that potent spirit of the Indies, was the one drink that had come to be regarded as equal to any situation, fair weather or foul. Anything less was considered little short of 'playactin'!

It was so with a sailing vessel. For many years prior to the twenties, most of the sail-minded world had been enthralled by the races for the *America's Cup*, a continuing contest begun in 1851 when the original race for a 100-Guineas Trophy, round the Isle of Wight, was won by the *America*—by a fluke, according to the Lunenburgers. They contended her shallower draught had enabled her to shorten the distance of the course by a full nine miles.

They hotly insisted she could hardly be called a deepwater boat; nor could any of those succeeding craft that year after year contended with each other for the Cup that had come to be known by her name. For the schoonerman's money, they were all of the same ilk, whether they sported the name of *Valkyrie*, *Shamrock*, *Resolute*, *Vanite* or *Defiance*. They were 'yachts' manned by 'yachtsmen,' forever being towed in for repairs and 'adjustments' of one kind or another. And when a 23-knot wind caused the New York Yacht Club to postpone a race in 1919, the snort of derision could be heard from Newfoundland to Gloucester!

After *that*, the demand for a series of races between honest-to-god sail carriers gathered like an August gale. It was answered by William H. Dennis, who announced through his newspaper, the Halifax *Herald*, that an elimination contest for schooners would be sailed off Halifax in October. The winner would challenge the best boat the Gloucestermen could lay hands on; at stake would be a brand new International Trophy as well as a cash prize. But—and this was more like it, agreed the Lunenburgers—any contender must be a bona-fide fisherman, with at least one trip to Newfoundland's Grand Banks to her credit. This stipulation was a prime part of the deed of gift to the Trophy.

The news beat up and down the coast to be quaffed like a swig of overproof rum by Yankee and Maritimes deep-water fishermen alike. Here was no namby-pamby, champagne competition but, at long last, a guarantee of the ultimate in pitting crew against crew, skipper against skipper, full-sailed hull against hull, and the devil take the weather!

More than a hundred sail made up the Lunenburg fleet alone. There was no lack of contenders and no quarter would be expected or offered among them in the process of deciding the men and the boats best-qualified to achieve victory. The arguments as to who was the best skipper and who had the smartest hull flew fast and furious with the name of Angus Walters, who was known for getting the best out of any bottom he sailed, being mentioned with increasing frequency. Still, it was agreed the selection must be fair; based upon something much more solid than opinion. An elimination contest alone could assure this. No less than eight schooners were readied.

The International Fishing Schooner Competitions—destined to be both a delight and a source of argument to gatherings of folk, inland and seaboard, American and Canadian, for the next twenty years—had begun. And thus too was born the story of the *Bluenose*, even though a full year was to pass before she would rise on

Newfoundland-born Ben Pine,
skippered Gloucester schooners
COLUMBIA and GERTRUDE L. THEBAUD —
BLUENOSE's ablest rivals in
the International Fishermen's Races.

(left) — Scene aboard BLUENOSE
during the heat of a race
as hands surge on topsail halyard.

(below) — BLUENOSE crewmen crowd
the rail as their vessel trails the
MARGARET K. SMITH
before the start of a single
elimination race held October 7, 1922,
off Halifax. BLUENOSE won the
contest and right to defend
the trophy she had won the previous
year from ELSIE.

Perhaps the most thrilling photograph of BLUENOSE racing.
With started sheets and lee rail under,
she reaches toward the finish line and victory.

the ways of a Lunenburg shipyard. If the legend of the *Bluenose* occupied a couple of decades, the 'keel' of her saga was laid that day in 1920, when Billy Dennis unveiled his proposal and offered the trophy for international competition.

It was now only a matter of time before *Bluenose* would begin the sail to her glory, defend her honours, carve her own unique place in the hearts of her admirers, glow in the limelight, languish in obscurity—and finally, perish in the pangs of lowly labour. If *Bluenose* and her legend would fade for a time, the image she was to fashion never would suffer that final eclipse, even when she slipped beneath the waves. The tale of her exploits and triumphs would lose some of its glamour for a time, but not its right to be remembered.

To this day, countless visitors to her home port ask where they can see something of the great ship. Invariably they offer their condolences to the townsfolk on their folly and their loss when they allowed her to slip from their hands to an ignominious end on a Caribbean reef. Just as he never seems to tire in the hearing, so the true Lunenburger fails to grow weary in the telling of the days, so long ago now, when the white-winged shapes of two lusty schooners against the sky—one of them always *Bluenose*—was the most thrilling sight the world had to offer.

Was *Bluenose* planned and built to be the Queen she ultimately became? How many races did she actually win? Was she ever beaten? Did she become slower with age? What was the secret of *Bluenose*? Was it her design? The sailing ability of her crew? Or was it the shrewdness and know-how of her captain?

And then, the most intriguing question of all: Was *Bluenose* a *freak*, the product of some unrecorded sorcery through a change made secretly during her building? The questions—like the answers—are endless. The truth lies only in the telling of the whole story, complete, factual and unbiased, and just as it happened—beginning with that Fall of 1920, before *Bluenose* herself yet had become even a gleam in the eye of her builders.

Came the first elimination contest. The eight schooners began a course laid out to test the rival boats on all points of sailing. The breeze was a sprightly twenty knots as the *Delawana*, under the hand of Captain Tommy Himmelman, and the *Gilbert B. Walters*, skippered by Captain Angus Walters, headed home from the last buoy. They were neck and neck.

Then, the *Gilbert B.* carried away her foretopmast and dropped steadily astern in spite of every effort to remain a contender. The *Delawana* crossed the finish line better than five minutes ahead to win the race, but in the eyes of most spectators Angus carried the day by reason of his canny seamanship.

Meanwhile, there was more sail-hustling in New England as the Gloucestermen held *their* elimination trials, resulting in a win by a small but smart schooner named the *Esperanto*, captained by Marty Welch. A whitewashed Yankee, they called Welch, who hailed originally from Digby, Nova Scotia. In a series of two races held off Halifax later that year, his *Esperanto* took both races without much trouble. Back she sailed to Gloucester with the International Trophy and a cash prize of $4,000. *Delawana*'s consolation of $1,000 in cash did little to assuage the dismay and chagrin of the Canadians, though they admitted the races had been fair and square to all parties. Now they needed a new schooner, to be designed and built with the double view of producing both a successful fisherman and a sailer able to trim the best the Americans might have to offer.

The name of William J. Roue, designer of the *Bluenose*, and that of her doughty captain, Angus Walters, have long been famous in the annals of maritime lore. The lustre surrounding both figures began and grew as the *Bluenose* herself worked to windward of illustrious fortune. But, strangely enough, it has remained for latter years and the addition of other conspicuous accomplishments to gild the name of the shipyard which built the great ship. Other hands trained her, but the hands of her builders created the prodigy of wind and sail.

George Rhuland and Richard D. Smith opened their shipbuilding yard in the heyday of the saltbank trade. They prospered in more ways than one—not least from Nova Scotia skippers and fishing firms who grew confident that Smith and Rhuland could produce a boat that would be the equal of all demands laid upon her. In those days, the naval architect seldom was much in the picture when a company or a master-mariner decided to have a schooner built. More often than not, the lines were laid down by the yard's partners, after long and frequent consultation with the prospective owners.

As the years passed, the design of the fishing schooner changed greatly. Through experience, the master of a planned hull knew exactly what he wanted, and any changes from the orthodox he wished to make. He could readily produce suggestions for adjustments in line and design he knew would make his new boat 'point' better (or work more smartly to windward). George Rhuland and Dick Smith were quick to see and apply any such advantage whenever they felt they 'knew it for a fact.' But they also could draw on an immense amount of know-how through the past experiences of generations of Lunenburg skippers who had found that this or that idea did or did not work out as hoped.

It's fair to say then, that when *Bluenose* came to be built, the sponsors had chosen a yard able to assure their dreams. After careful consultation between all parties, a keel was laid for the new schooner in the Smith and Rhuland yard. In a colorful ceremony, a golden spike was driven into it by Canada's Governor-General, the Duke of Devonshire . . . or at least, such was the general intention. But that august gentleman arrived too early for the act and was borne off for an interlude of suitable libation until the moment should arrive for him to do his stuff. In the process, he fell among friends indeed; when he returned, serene in soul but not of eye, he completely missed with his first swing of the iron maul—much to the mortification of the stuffier spectators. His aim did not improve with practice. Someone finally took pity and drove the errant spike home for him.

A moment later, veteran shipwrights who had fashioned no less than 119 vessels fell happily to work and *Bluenose* began to take shape on the ways that nearly forty years later were to cradle the movie ship *Bounty*, and not long after, the replica of the schooner herself, as *Bluenose II*. On that day too, began the long and proud history of the Smith and Rhuland yard as it was to relate to famous ships, and its emergence into world fame.

Bill Roue had done his work well. He had drawn into his plans innovations and details calculated to produce a winner. Among other things, to keep the inside ballast as low as possible, he stipulated the top of the keel be reinforced with iron-impregnated concrete. Later on, with his consent, the yard made an alteration in his plans by raising the freeboard in the bow by eighteen inches, to provide more headroom in the fo'c's'le in response to a demand by the owners. This change, it has been contended, enabled her to work better to wind-

ward, and it may be so, for *Bluenose* always was a dry ship in any sea.

The change also resulted in the hull sporting 'cheeks,' a feature that sharply distinguished her from other schooners, and undoubtedly brought about the slight angle in the line traced by her bow-stem. But the most careful investigation has established clearly that no other change was made, either by caprice or plan. As Fred Rhuland, now Secretary-Treasurer of the yard, has said, "No reputable yard-master would dare to make any change without confirming it in advance with the owners. The *Bluenose* was quite definitely no freak. Probably, the main reason for her remarkable sailing abilities lay in the fact that she was what we call a 'lean' ship. With a total length of 143 feet and a straight keel measurement of only 50 feet, almost two-thirds of her was overhang and this surely gave her much of her great speed."

The schooner was launched March 26, 1921, amid great hopes and appropriate celebration. Yet hardly one of the many hundreds of onlookers could have had any idea he was witnessing the birth of a legend that nippy Lunenburg morning. It's equally certain that neither of the two builder-partners could possibly have anticipated what an aura of fame would some day surround their yard.

The *Bluenose* was built almost entirely of Nova Scotia wood—spruce, oak, birch and pine . . . except for her masts of Oregon pine. She matured to beauty as ballast was poured in to 'bring her down' properly, and her masts stepped to tower well over a hundred-and-score feet above her deck. The riggers completed their part of the job quickly and well. By April 15, she was ready to sail from the harbour on sea trials, paced by two other schooners. A short time later she cleared for the Banks. When at the end of summer she returned to port, heavy-laden, she had established herself beyond all doubt as a fisherman. Already, she was undisputed highliner of the fleet.

It didn't take long to ready *Bluenose* for her first elimination trials off Halifax that fall. She was hauled out, her working booms and fishing sails were removed, running gear was overhauled and topmasts were set. Sporting a spanking new coat of paint, she arrived in Halifax on Saturday, October 8, 1921. The city went wild over this nautical prima donna with the look of a champion. Tall-sparred, lean-hulled and bearing more than 10,000 square feet of canvas, she was something to stop the

ELSIE, Gloucester defender of the International Fishermen's Cup,
follows BLUENOSE home at the finish of the 1921 contest.
During the race, in setting her ballooner, ELSIE lost her foretopmast.
Here, it is seen lashed to the foremast.
ELSIE was lost in 1935 off St. Pierre.

breath of even the most land-lubbered observer.

"How'll she do, Cap'n?" roared a questioner to Angus from the wharf.

"She's a wery good wessel," was the quiet reply.

The following Saturday morning, six schooners jockeyed about the starting line with *Bluenose*. Hailing from Lunenburg, from Shelburne and LaHave, they finally got away in the following order:

SHIP	MASTER	TIME
Bluenose	Angus Walters	10.30.35
Independence	Albert Himmelman	10.31.09
J. Duffy	Spindler	10.31.10
Canadia	J. Conrad	10.31.30
Alcala	Roland Knickle	10.31.45
Ada R. Corkum	Corkum	10.33.22
Donald J. Cook	Cook	10.33.55
Delawana	Backman	10.34.15

The race started in a mere seven-and-three-quarter-knot breeze, which soon freshened to twelve knots as the three leaders rounded the First Mark—*Bluenose*, followed by *Canadia*, then *Alcala*.

A bank of fog, descending with the speed and manner of a London pea-souper, suddenly and completely wiped out all chance for the boats to observe each other's movements. It also obscured observation of the race from shore.

"Der name o' God," grumbled a *Bluenose* crewman, suitably fortified with rum and the knowledge that many of the crew's womenfolk were watching the race from the nearest shoreline, "If only our vives knew vair vere ve!"

"Ta hell vit our vives," growled a shipmate "If only ve knew vair vere ve ourselves!"

But, as often happens, as suddenly as it had appeared, the fog lifted. The schooners reached for the Southeast Automatic Buoy, six miles away. *Bluenose* rounded it ahead of *Alcala*—and then went off on the windward thresh of some nine miles to the Sambro Lightship. The wind, rising to twenty knots, provided a first-class test of ships, crews and skippers. *Bluenose* had demonstrated her superiority off the wind; now, to windward, she ran like a scared rabbit. She led round the Third Mark, then scurried down to finish. It was an easy win.

Angus Walters himself had steered his new schooner to her first victory. In races during the next seventeen years, he would seldom trust her helm to anyone else.

The second race was again the story of the first. When *Bluenose* came on the wind, although beaten to the Sambro Lightship by *Delawana*, she went to weather and was not headed again. She had beaten *Canadia* in the first race by over four minutes. In the second, she had bested her nearest rival, *Delawana*, by better than fifteen minutes. She had won the right to challenge the Americans for the International Trophy.

Before the first international contest involving *Bluenose* could take place, a wrangle began that was to smoulder in the fo'c's'les of both sides long after the rulings were made. Word reached Halifax that the American Race Committee had chosen *Mayflower* of Boston, undeniably a plain-and-simple *yacht*, to defend against the Canadian challenger, and the Nova Scotians were having none of her. They were accused of being afraid of the trim new Yankee craft; they hotly denied this was the case at all. *Mayflower* was no saltbanker, they declared, but a vessel that had been designed expressly for racing, with little if any thought to her capabilities as a working fisherman.

Still more outrageous, she was not owned by a commercial fishing concern and even the legend "Schooner-Yacht" appeared on her sail plan! If anyone really wanted to know, they *were* scared, but not of *Mayflower* herself; rather of the International Schooner Races lapsing into a pithy repeat of the *America's Cup* set-up, with this 'yacht' becoming the thin edge of the wedge that would lead to the end of contests between bona-fide schooners.

The Americans sent a representative to Halifax to argue their case, but the Canadians were adamant. So a meeting of the Trustees was held. The Americans were formally notified that *Mayflower* was ineligible, according to the Deed of Trust. Here was a pretty kettle of fish for United States interests . . . and nothing to do about it! They took the only course open to them and speedily arranged an elimination contest among their boats, from which the schooner *Elsie* emerged the winner. She arrived in Halifax amid great fanfare and prepared to take on her Canadian opponent. *Bluenose* had made a quick trip to Lunenburg, following the Canadian elimination series, to have her bottom gone over. When she returned, *Elsie* was waiting and ready.

Ironically enough, on her way up from Lunenburg, *Bluenose* fell in with a stranger . . . none other than the Boston pride, *Mayflower*!

Sporting the champion's number "ONE" on her mainsail for the first time,
BLUENOSE trails in HENRY FORD'S lee
off Gloucester, October, 1922,
at the start of a race hampered by light airs. BLUENOSE took the series.
FORD went to the bottom off Newfoundland six years later.

The Canadian challenger was reaching for Pennant Point and the American decided to give her a go. She fell behind the new Lunenburger consistently, but while this was not the Nova Scotia ship's best point of sailing, neither was the Boston boat being pushed, and the short sprint was not taken as a fair assessment of the merits of either ship.

On Saturday, October 22, a twenty-five knot wind blessed the start of the first race between *Bluenose* and *Elsie*. The New Englander was skippered by Capt. Marty Welch, later to be named by Angus as the best all-round master of the American challengers. Marty had the better of Angus as they crossed the line, but the Lunenburger luffed the Gloucesterman into the calm under Sandwich Point and managed to lead him by a narrow margin over the first legs of the course. Now Angus was feeling out his vessel, trying first one sail pattern, then another. Finally he tried a ballooner, and his new *Bluenose* responded like a greyhound! Marty followed suit, but in setting his ballooner, carried away his foretopmast. Promptly, Angus showed his good sportsmanship. He not only doused his ballooner, but thereafter carried even less sail than the Yankee skipper. With the wind blowing great guns, both schooners raced for the finish line. *Bluenose*, scuppers awash, crossed at 1.32.10. *Elsie* followed at 1.45.25, and that was that!

After the race, a *Bluenose* crewman spotted Mrs. Marty Welch, wife of *Elsie*'s skipper, who had watched the contest from a Halifax pier.

"Vell now Mrs. Welch, it's a pity the *Elsie* didn't win that race," the fisherman consoled. "And you know, *Elsie* vould've von if it veren't for something in the vater today."

"Really? What was in the water?" asked the woman. The fisherman allowed himself a devilish smile. "*The Bluenose!*"

Bluenose had shown an obvious superiority that day on all points. Moreover, she accentuated it the whole of the way in the second race on Monday. *Elsie*, sporting brand new topmasts, was still no match for the speedy Lunenburger. She came to the finish line more than three miles behind!

An interesting side light of the series had occurred during the second race when *Mayflower* showed up on the course to sail along unofficially. Hardly in racing rig, for she was carrying only her four lowers, she was in no shape to show her mettle. She was overshadowed too by *Delawana*, equally adorned

in canvas, who also put in an appearance during the contest, to join in the unqualified fun.

The rejoicing in Halifax and along the coast that autumn night can well be imagined. Aboard *Bluenose*, a joyful crewman did a jig, proposed they all "tie one on" and begged "the borry of a chaw" off a fellow crew member—all in one breath. "Great jumpin' codfish, Bingie," growled his exasperated shipmate, "don't you ever *buy* any?" Then, resigning himself to the inevitable, he dug a huge ham of a hand down through dripping oilskins, bent double, plumbed the depths of an inner pocket and rummaged searchingly about in the region of his crotch. Finally he straightened and brought forth a virgin plug of the dank, dark chewing tobacco so beloved of the saltbank fisherman. A moment later he got it back from the pan-handler and gazed ruefully at the bit that remained.

"Bingie," he cautioned, "You'll likely find det a leedle damp this mornin'. I don't hold my vater like I used tuh."

Thus ended the first International Series in which *Bluenose* was a contender. It set her up as the acknowledged champion as well as the boat to beat, and the story of the International Fishermen's Races from that date forward becomes a chronicle of rivals' efforts to achieve the impossible.

THE 1921 SERIES ENDED as *Bluenose* and her Lunenburg crew returned to the Banks to fish, and the Americans to Gloucester to plan for the 1922 series, determined to come up with a boat that would take the Champion. They went straight to work. Captain Thomas McManus, a noted producer of fleet schooners, was given the job of designing a ship to turn the trick.

The result was the *Henry Ford*, and not a man among those who looked her over could doubt her sweet lines would provide what it would take. Unfortunately, she was so badly damaged in launching that she could not possibly get in a qualifying trip to the Banks before race time. The Board of Trustees granted a special dispensation, since her design conformed to the regulations, and allowed that she be repaired during the time she should normally have been fishing.

This brought a prompt submission from the owners of *Mayflower*, who pointed out that their boat now had put in a summer and winter

*COLUMBIA, cited by Angus Walters as "finest of the American contenders",
lost a hard-fought series to BLUENOSE, lodged a protest at technical sailing
error by latter. Four years later, the beautiful Gloucester schooner took her
22 seamen to the bottom in a Sable Island gale.*

of fishing, thus providing her eligibility. Nevertheless, the Lunenburgers held to their original contention, at the same time noting their non-opposition to the *Ford* as proof of their good faith. The Trustees likewise refused to reverse their decision of 1921, but they condescended to explain why. It was, they said, not only her design, or her type of construction, or even her ownership that ruled out the *Mayflower*. But her now-completed fishing trips had served only to confirm that she *was* a "fresh" fisherman, and wholly incapable in the saltfishing trade. They reiterated that she had been designed with a major view to racing, and in no way conformed to the requirements for development of a schooner ideally adapted to the industry as both a sailer and a worker.

"The Committee was scared of us racing the *Mayflower*," Angus said later, "though I would have been quite happy to do so. I had a good look at her on the marine railway once, and I knew then she'd be no trouble for us. I told them so, but they stuck to their guns."

And so it was that *Henry Ford* and not the *Mayflower* went into the elimination races off Gloucester, October 12 and 14, 1922. Having handily defeated the *Yankee* and the *L.A. Dunton*, both of Boston, as well as the *Elizabeth Howard* out of New York, she made ready to set sail against the pride of the Canadians in a series scheduled to open October 21, off *Ford*'s home port.

(*Bluenose* had met three other Nova Scotia schooners off Halifax on Saturday, October 7, in a single elimination race. Neither the *Canadia*, the *Mahaska*, nor the *Margaret K. Smith* was "in it." *Bluenose* took the victory, hands down.)

The light airs of an October morning caressed the sails of the two schooners standing at the starting line, hoping to trap any errant breeze that came along. Spirits were keen and all hands got ready to test once and for all the opinions, discussions and contentions that had raged, ashore and afloat, for these many months. Aboard the Committee Boat, decision was reached to postpone the start for thirty minutes in the belief that the breeze would freshen. The postponement signal was accordingly hoisted. But the rival skippers had decided to take matters into their own hands. Standing almost close enough to the American boat to permit passing a bucket of bait, Angus hailed his opponent.

"How about it, Clayt?"

"Okay by me," came the reply from Clayton Morrisey, captain of the *Ford*, and the race was in the works.

Seeing its signal ignored, the Committee fired a shot to record its consternation and to accentuate the postponement order. When this failed, the Canadian destroyer which had convoyed *Bluenose* from Nova Scotia was dispatched to megaphone the two Captains that the start had been delayed. There was no response. Crews and skippers alike had waited too long for this moment and were in no mood to be denied it. Both schooners kept on running down the first leg, although "limping" would be a better word.

The day brought no sign of wind. *Bluenose* trailed *Ford*, who proved to be a light sailer, all the way around the course. Neither boat managed to finish within the time limit.

"Chalk one up for Clayt," Angus admitted as he stepped ashore. The Judges had other thoughts, and they declared, "No race."

The crew of the *Ford* went wild, and who could wonder why? Both skippers had agreed to start and they had worked like dogs all day trying one sail pattern after another—and for what? As far as they were concerned, the Committee could go to hell, time limit or no time limit. They would call it quits at once unless the race was allowed.

Fortunately, wiser heads prevailed. Best cooling agent among them was Josephus Daniels, then Secretary of the United States Navy, who appealed to predominant elements in the *Ford*'s crew originally hailing from the south shore of Nova Scotia.

"Never let it be said," he begged, "that the men of the Pubnico's and Clark's Harbor were the ones to trail 'Old Glory' in the dust."

That did it! Back the schooners went to the starting line. The winds were appallingly light, but not quite so ineffective as they had been the first day. Both contenders managed to finish within the time limit of six hours and the *Henry Ford* rode proudly in the van—though by a scant two minutes and twenty-six seconds.

The second race was quite another story. The wind had blown almost constantly at a respectable twenty knots. Halfway around, preparing to come about, the *Ford*, like *Elsie* the year before, carried away her foretopmast. Strangely enough, she seemed to do even better without it, but she never headed *Bluenose*, who crossed the finish line well in the lead. She finished on the mark of 4.57.41 to the *Henry Ford's* of 5.05.04.

Ashore in Gloucester, some few remnant die-hards of America's Cup ilk complained loudly that weather that would take the topmast out of the *Ford* was unfit for racing. To the credit of her crew, they did not join in this contention, figuring all's fair in sail and gale.

"The *Ford* was kind of tender-sided," Angus once recalled of the challenger. "I never could figure it out, but something Gloucester never seemed to learn was not to over-canvas their vessels. Practically all that I saw carried too much sail and that made them tender weather boats."

In the third and deciding contest, with the wind blowing a fine twenty-five knot breeze, *Bluenose* won without the slightest trouble, leaving no doubt in anyone's mind which was the better boat, nicely defending her title and sailing home with the cash award. Her finish time in the final race was 4.48.38, with the *Henry Ford's*, 4.56.29. In each contest she had shown herself to be vastly superior on all points of sailing.

As Angus stepped ashore in Lunenburg, he met with customary aplomb the question of how rough it had been that day the *Ford* lost her foretopmast.

"Well, I'll tell you," he said, "I never wore no coat or oilskins and if there was any spray flyin' I never felt it. 'Course there *was* some water around, where we was sloshin' her down to keep her cool on the deck."

Then, as he walked away shaking his head: "Certainly not the kind of weather you look for a topmast to go in. Leastaways, ours didn't."

IF THERE WAS ANY ONE of the American challengers to *Bluenose* which gained the grudging, even unreserved, admiration of the Canadian schoonermen, that boat was *Columbia*. And small wonder! She was about as pretty a thing as anyone could want to behold.

She came from the board of W. Starling Burgess, acknowledged as probably the greatest American designer of his day, and imbued with a burning desire to achieve what no one else so far even had come close to: the humbling of *Bluenose*. He had designed *Mayflower* and he needed no reminder of the importance of qualifications. This time there would be no question of the boat being a true schooner; he came up with a design that left no doubt of her ability to operate as a saltbanker. Just

for good measure, he had drawn her smart enough to fill the role of a fresh fisherman, as well.

She came down the ways with the sweet sort of look to her lines which, even before rigging, was enough to worry the Canadians. Her lean, sleek bow rode high, just like *Bluenose*, and she looked like something designed for no other reason but to personify the very essence of speed itself.

The American Committee had already picked her to challenge and in the meantime she had put in a season on the Banks. But she spruced up and entered an elimination contest. Meeting the *Ford* and the old *Howard* in a race sailed in extremely light wind, she showed them both a clean pair of heels. Though the contest was not finished by any of the three boats within the time limit, she was far ahead of the *Ford* by the time the race was called. Soon after, she set out for Halifax for her bout with the Canadian Champion. She found *Bluenose* waiting and eager to do battle.

American authorities had contacted Angus Walters to discover whether he would object to Gloucester shipowner Ben Pine skippering their challenger. The race rules stipulated that the master of a challenger, like the vessel herself, had to be a working fisherman. It seemed that Pine, who was a chief investor in the Gloucester fleet, did not sail with any of his vessels to the fishing grounds.

Angus had known Ben for years. "He'll do fine," he said.

Race number one was scheduled for Monday, October 29. A breeze of about seventeen knots was a-blowing. *Columbia*, whose appearance claimed much favorable comment in the Nova Scotia capital, was understood to go like a startled deer in this sort of weather. But *Bluenose* too was anything but unhappy. Trimmed somewhat lighter in ballast than in previous contests, she handled as sprightly as her rival in the moderate wind.

The lead of thirty seconds that Angus wrung out of the start was dissipated when he overstood the Second Mark, allowing *Columbia's* master, Ben Pine, to race him neck-and-neck all the way to the Third Buoy. They reached it in a dead heat. There followed what probably became the most talked of duel in the annals of the International Series—an out-and-out fight for the weather berth as, bow to bow, Pine pressed his advantage of position to force Angus to green water inside the mark. With all his cunning, the scrappy little Lunenburg skipper sought to shake off his tormentor; but Ben Pine hung on like a leech.

By now, *Bluenose* was within spittin' distance of the "Three Sisters" ledge, ominous both in fact and prospect. A roar from pilot to helmsman on *Bluenose* to bear away or strike the shoal brought an instant reply; the alternative was to ram *Columbia!* Squarely between the devil and the deep, Angus gambled on collision. *Bluenose* bore away from the ledge. Pine held to his course.

Immediately, Angus doused his staysail and swung his foresail to make her "wing and wing." A few seconds later, his main boom struck the mainshrouds of *Columbia*, travelled forward to sweep the Yankee's forestays and finally snarled in his jib, impudently towing the challenger for almost a full minute.

But that was it! *Bluenose* cleared suddenly and took off for home like all the hounds of hell were baying in her wake, crossing the line with a time of 1.43.42 to *Columbia's* 1.45.02. Scant margin, but a clean win. Clearly, the Lunenburgers had had good reason to worry at the prospect of *Columbia*!

The night that followed bred arguments fast and furious. Ben Pine hadn't fought fair when he angled Angus toward the rocks. . . Angus was subject to protest by Pine because of the unofficial minute's "tow." It *was* a point for rules, no denying—if anyone wanted to attempt applying them; but nothing could be further from the mind of either skipper, both of whom seemed to be in equal jeopardy. Both masters ignored the point. They looked to the next race to provide a more definite settlement on which was the better contender.

There was no wind on the Tuesday following and the race was cancelled. On Wednesday morning, two disconsolate *Bluenose* crewmen squatted on the after-rail bemoaning the continued absence of the slightest breeze for a start. One, whittling a small stick furiously, paused abruptly and peered closely at a tiny beetle that came in for a landing on his handiwork.

"Albert, come o'er here," he demanded—and when his shipmate obliged, "What kinda bug is det?"

Albert allowed himself a brief glance.

"Good God, Dutchie, don't you know vat det is? Det's a lady-bug!"

"It is!" Dutchie shook his head in wonder . . . then turned a look of open admiration on his companion. "By der Khwrrist, Albert, you got some pair o' *eyes* on yuh!"

"Yeah, and I got qvite a nose on me too— for vind! Dere's a breeze comin'!"

And there was: a mere eight-knotter — but still, a breeze! Enough for only a start — or so the Committee thought when they called off the proceedings. But Albert's nose was not to be denied its cunning; the wind confounded all and sundry by almost immediately freshening to something much heavier. Both ships gained way and kept on,—unofficially, of course.

Columbia, reballasted and lighter than ever, was well out in front at the moment of the call-off, but with the stronger breeze, *Bluenose* quickly put such nonsense to rout. At race's end, she was already tied up snug and proper at the dock when *Columbia* reached hers!

Next day's race was official. The schooners started off in a hearty twenty-five-knot blow. Spectators, crews and skippers, knew they were in for "something like." Fact is, the whole series of that year proved to be a "real one," with each race—like the first— offering never a dull moment! In part at least, this was because of what had happened in the wake of the initial heat.

The judges decided to draw up a roster of rules to apply in future, including one which decreed that henceforth all buoys on the course were to be passed *to seaward*. The decision was made because the earlier race had demonstrated so clearly the hazards threatening competitors forced into shallow water in order to pass inside a buoy. Little did Angus realize how vital would become the observance of this rule to the letter!

Once again besting *Columbia* at the start, the Lunenburg Captain raced for the inner Automatic, passing inside the Lighthouse Bank buoy, which, as he was well aware (too aware as it proved) had been shifted into the fairway for use as an examination stop-mark during the First World War. Pine, on the other hand, passed as stipulated to seaward of the buoy. Then, both schooners tore off for the Second Mark and on to the finish. *Bluenose* crossed two minutes and forty-five seconds ahead of her rival.

Angus tied up; the heady glow of total victory about his brow. He had saved the Trophy in two straight races and his crew was already talking of the celebrations that would surely crown their return to Lunenburg. But his joy was shortlived. Almost immediately he was advised that Ben Pine had lodged a protest. He claimed Angus illegally passed to port of a buoy. The *Bluenose* skipper's anger passed all bounds when he was further told that the Committee, after long and serious consideration, had declared the race "forfeit" to *Columbia* and announced the Series stood at one-all. He declared neither he nor his crew would abide by such a ruling. He was going home!

A warning that such action was likely to mean forfeiture of the Series failed to deter him; he was in no mood to submit to a threat.

"Look," he said, now with deadly calm, "Ben knows as well as I do that that there buoy don't mean nothing on this race course. It never did! It was put there, as everybody knows, during the War—not as a shoal buoy, but as a stop-point marker for customs inspection. Now, we both sailed through the same amount of water—and who crossed the finish line first? Tell me that! Ben very well knows he couldn't beat us, so what's all this talk about buoys?"

Still, he insisted, he didn't want to be unreasonable. Let the Committee declare "no race," instead of handing it to *Columbia* "on a silver platter," and he would be willing to continue the Series.

The judges appealed to Arthur Zwicker, president of the Bluenose Company, to try and break the impasse. Zwicker admitting the error, albeit technical, prepared to scout for another crew to sail *Bluenose* in a third race scheduled for Saturday, in case Angus would not relent. It was a fatal move, taken without figuring on the little Captain's resourcefulness, who, Zwicker had forgotten, was not only skipper, but managing owner of the schooner as well. The mere suggestion of a scratch crew with another master was all Angus needed. He roared an order to cast off and set course for home.

Since Ben Pine refused to sail *Columbia* around the course by her lonesome, in order to claim the Trophy, the Committee called it quits, ruled that neither skipper had won the day, and awarded half the prize money to the Americans. And so ended International Racing for a full eight years. In its stead, Lunenburg interests proceeded to beguile themselves with attempts to come up with a vessel of their own that might take the measure of their own Champion.

The first of these was *Mahaska*, built by rule of thumb, and equipped with a superstitious magic thought to be evoked through a name containing three "A's". Seemingly, the name proved to be all she had; she was no match at all for the *Bluenose*.

Now came the *Haligonian*, designed by— of all people—Bill Roue, who understandably was seeking to demonstrate *who* had been primarily responsible for the success of the now famous schooner.

Haligonian was "a big one" all right, as dimensions went, but she sported a deckline as straight as a tuna's backbone. Instead of riding the swells like *Bluenose*, she plowed straight through them. In a race with any wind at all, there was not a dry bone to be found in any man-jack of her crew. Launched in 1925, she put in a couple of seasons on the Banks and turned up for a specially arranged Series with *Bluenose* on October of 1926. She handled badly from the start. She had struck in the Straight of Canso when, her owners claimed, she had been "hogged," and she carried a lee helm. But *Bluenose*, too, had once been ashore on the coast of Newfoundland. What's more, she had barely weathered a severe battering in a Sable Island gale; any quarter *Haligonian* might have claimed would have been laughed off.

The two Lunenburgers finally met at the starting line, four times in all. Race number one saw *Haligonian* finish so far astern as to be out of view to the men on the *Bluenose!* The next two contests were not completed within the time limit, owing to unusually light winds. Race number four saw *Bluenose* cross the line a good seven minutes in the van.

If Lunenburgers ever had had any hopes they might of themselves produce a better vessel than their proven Champion, these now vanished, never to return. *Bluenose* went back to fishing; her racing crew to more rewarding pursuits. So passed, at least for a time, the heart-skipping sight of two white-mantled hulls, straining to vanquish each other, each under the hand of a master-sailor and the eyes of half a world.

Gertrude L. Thebaud WAS HER NAME. She was small and she was winsome. If ever a schooner looked fleet and lovely, it was *Thebaud!* She bore herself with the air of a Boston debutante—strictly Back Bay Boston—and well she might; she was that city's presentation piece in the high-seas court of international sailing rivalry. Since Gloucester's hardy fishermen had not been able to conquer *Bluenose*, the

Brahmins of the city of famous tea parties had decided to give it a go. *Thebaud* bespoke the fact that they were going to make a real try of it while they were about it!

She was built at Essex, Massachusetts, this pretty craft on which so many hopes of Yankee-land were laid, and as fate would have it, she was destined to be the one vessel to defeat *Bluenose*—not in the old Canadian International Series to be sure, where her sponsors would much have preferred it to happen, but in a Series specially arranged for October, 1930. Still, defeat is defeat, no matter in what guise it's met.

The indefatigable Sir Thomas Lipton— he of the never-say-die, never-ending attempts to lift the *America's Cup*—had been approached to offer a trophy for international schooner competition, and he readily agreed. Off went a challenge to Lunenburg, that found *Bluenose* once more immersed in her trade. Like nothing so much as an old fish-wife who gathers her skirts to race from garden-patch to house at news of an intruder, she unfurled a spanking new suit of sails and went hurrying down to Boston to answer this latest, impudent threat to her good name.

By this time, she was old, and just a little tired of proving her mettle. But she was still game! On October 9, she sidled up alongside her junior rival and crossed the starting line one minute and ten seconds behind *Thebaud*, captained by Angus' friendly old foe, Ben Pine. From the word go, Angus had trouble. The new sails on *Bluenose*, stretched almost beyond belief during her run down the coast, made her sluggish. Try as he could, he was able to do little better than flop twice around the eighteen mile triangular course, to finish 12 minutes and 37 seconds behind the American challenger.

Quickly sail-makers went to work on those over-sized sails. Angus, who claimed no quarter, also repaired a section of loosened keel to better his chances and promised a much improved showing in the second race.

"She's not at her best, that's sure," he said, "but someone has to win—and it's not over yet!"

But that Saturday, with *Bluenose* acting much smarter, the race had to be called in a falling wind. The following Monday it was again the same story, with *Bluenose* out in front when the race was called. Tuesday saw practically no wind at all; postponement again was declared and the men on both ships called on whatever gods there be to "fetch up a leedle blow."

There's said to be an old-time cure for calm; time-honoured of sailors the world over. Like most superstitions of the sea, you either believe it or you don't. Aboard the Canadian Government boat, on hand to carry the Committee and members of the press around the course in the wake of the racing schooners, Agnes McGuire, Canadian newspaper woman and former Lunenburger, felt the situation called for any remedy to hand, superstition or not. She recalled the oft-time declarations of fishermen that sometimes the only way to get wind was to "buy" it! Gathering up every last coin in her change-purse, as the Committee Boat came in to tie up at the wharf, she walked to the rail and flung the offering into the water, adding a fervent prayer for the morrow. When, on Wednesday, the day dawned in a real blow, who could say it was not because the deities of the sea had been properly importuned? Both schooners took off like a pair of unleashed hounds.

But now the judges decided the vessels could not pick up what Angus had scornfully referred to as the "baby buoys" on the course (and soon had cause to wish he hadn't) because of the gale that was blowing, and once again called off the race. Angus went wild with frustration. Who could blame him? In spite of the wind and weather that day, he had managed to make temporary repairs to a threstle-tree which carried away. A little later, with *Bluenose* heeled well over, an ear-splitting crack rent the air. The boom-jaws on the big mainsail had split, and the sail was in danger of being ripped clear.

"All hands to the main boom!" roared Angus, and the crew leapt to the task as one man. Tales of the legendary strength of Lunenburg sea captains were vindicated that day on the deck of *Bluenose*. In the teeth of a howling gale, every man straining might and main, the great boom was slowly, inexorably shipped back to butt against the mainmast, then lashed smartly into place!

"And," boasted one of them later, "Angus hadn't no need to bring her up, or spill no wind either, for us to do the job!"

Considering the mainsail represented some 4,000 square feet of wind-filled canvas, the accomplishment of such a task in the circumstances of the moment, testified to a tremendous show of muscle-power. But, the feat only

GERTRUDE L. THEBAUD was small, lithe and lovely. A heavy sail-carrier, fishermen knew her by her high-peaked main gaff. THEBAUD was the only challenger ever to defeat BLUENOSE, as she took the series for the Lipton Trophy off Gloucester in 1930. In the last two series for the International Fishermen's Trophy, she too bowed to the superior sailing qualities of the Canadian champion. THEBAUD was smashed to pieces on the breakwater at La Guaira, Venezuela, during a storm in 1948.

BLUENOSE leading THEBAUD.

added to the frustrated skipper's feeling of rage at the call-off, even though it meant a day to make permanent repairs.

The race on October 17 was called off for lack of wind, but Saturday provided a better breeze. In spite of moderate airs, *Bluenose* again took the lead. By the time the half-way mark was reached, she was a good five minutes ahead. Then Angus split tacks with his rival. It was a fatal move. He lost the favorable position he had established and *Thebaud* forged ahead, never to be headed.

Years later, Angus explained the reason for his mistake in that last race.

"Something I never liked to do when I raced the *Bluenose* was to take somebody else's advice. For that race, we had a New England pilot aboard. He told me that if I split tacks and stood in under the land, I'd catch a favourable wind from the nor'west. Well I did it, and instead, the wind got light, from the sou'-west, and dead ahead. We had trouble then because we were on a lee shore. I've often laid awake since wondering what got into me to make me take that fella's advice! Still and all,

it was certainly my mistake, and *Thebaud* made the best of it."

The news rang throughout America! It had finally been done; *Bluenose* had been bested! The smart little lady from Boston had managed the impossible. Proudly the victors received the Lipton Trophy and promptly they issued a challenge for the Canadian International Trophy in a Series to be sailed the following year, October of 1931. They would make a complete job of it!

Few there were, with any sense of true sportsmanship about them, who could begrudge the Americans their victory. Heaven knows they had striven too mightly and too often for it to be any less sweet for the circumstances surrounding it. But it was hard, too, for the Lunenburgers to accept defeat under those same facts. No question about it: *Bluenose* had lost the first race under conditions that ruled out the barest possibility of a win; the way her sails flapped about, stretched as they were beyond all reason, it was likely a mud-scow, rigged with jury-mast and staysail, could have given her competition. Then, in Wednesday's race, as early as the twelve-mile mark, she had forged a lead of two miles when the Sailing Committee had called the race—not for lack of wind (it had been blowing great guns)—but because the judges feared the abilities of the skippers to pick up those so-called "baby buoys!"

"Why don't they let us stay out there until something carries away?" raged Angus, in the light of one postponement after another. "We were perfectly satisfied to carry on!"

So were the Gloucestermen!

As for the race just finished, which had given *Thebaud* her second win, the Lunenburgers could not forget that *Bluenose* had established a five-minute lead at the eighteen-mile mark. The lead had been fairly lost, by reason of the decision Angus made to split tacks, but the result hardly could be taken to mean *Thebaud* was faster than *Bluenose*—not by the most biased of observers. As for one fair loss—the final race—well, *Bluenose* had dropped a race before this, but never a Series. For the Lunenburgers' money, this Series hadn't proved anything. They were more than eager for the next contest . . . the sooner the better!

The challenge so promptly sent out for the official Trophy indicated the Americans harboured somewhat similar feelings, in spite of their great and natural elation over the win. Little wonder then, that the Canadians accepted so readily, and arrangements were reached for a Series the next October. The Yankees were confident and eager. The Canadians were just as hot for another "go."

THE ABOUNDING ENTHUSIASM that greeted both schooners upon their arrival in Halifax that autumn of 1931 was coloured by the thought on the part of many that International Schooner Racing well could be approaching its final chapters. The marketing of fish was entering a phase of drastic changes and development from which hardly a stage in the industry was likely to escape. New methods of processing and merchandising were already beginning to lay huge demands on the supply. The methods for catching fish and rushing them to the family table in their freshest possible state were changing too. "Trawling" and "dragging," two ways of taking the catch in larger, vastly speedier fashion, were starting to supplant the traditional dory-set trawl lines. Already, hardly a sailing vessel in the fleets but had suffered the indignity of having

diesels installed; who could tell how long the end of the true schooner would be delayed?

As for *Bluenose*, time had wrought its change upon her too. She now was a full ten years old; there would be no shame if she should have to bow to so young and lively a rival as *Thebaud*, barely a year from the builder's hands. The old campaigner had absorbed so much of the sea itself that her water line measured two feet more than her design called for. When new, she had required some seventy tons of ballast; now she needed only fifty! Besides, as Angus explained, when she had lain on her side for a week in the gravel of Newfoundland's Placentia Bay, a year previously, something had happened to her; her starboard side must now be trimmed with ten tons more ballast than her port side.

The real wonder was that she still handled as she did; that she still looked as though she hadn't lost a single one of her sailing qualities. In fact, she seemed to be going better than ever, and she now proved it in the shortest order on record.

In the first race of the 1931 Series, *Bluenose* had been out in front of *Thebaud* by thirty-five minutes when the time allowance expired and the day ended without an official win. That was a Saturday. On Monday, with the wind still less than either Angus or Ben Pine wished for, she again crossed the finish line in comfort, an overwhelming thirty-two minutes ahead of the American boat. Indeed, at that point, *Thebaud* was not even in sight and repeated the embarrassment suffered by *Columbia* some years before by coming in to dock to find her conqueror already tied up, "snug-and-harbour-stowed."

Little wonder Angus couldn't deny himself impertinent comment to the press boys!

"You know, it was kinda lonely out there today," and his eyes twinkled. "*Thebaud* wasn't any company—in either race, for that matter— and a feller don't get much fun out o' racin' the clock all the time."

As for Captain Ben Pine, he could only make valiant efforts to bring his boat into better shape for racing. There was plenty to be done. He had taken on an extra ten-ton of ballast for the run down from Gloucester and there was no doubt it made *Thebaud* handle anything but smartly.

"It's not a case of misplaced ballast," he lamented. "It's simply too much ballast . . . and there are other things too. Her sails don't set like they should and she's plain sluggish. We've got to do something about all this, but I doubt if we can beat *Bluenose* this trick."

He was all too right. On Tuesday, *Bluenose* made it two straight by romping across the finish line a decisive eight minutes to the good.

That Series was more than enough to satisfy the Lunenburgers that *Thebaud* had never been a real threat to the record and reputation of their boat. They sailed home to Lunenburg to an uproarious victors' welcome as the town greeted them with band and victory parade to crown their heart-warming feat. Well they might, too, for a good seven years would pass before there again would be a similar opportunity. It was in the fall of 1938, when the next Series was held, and *Bluenose* was to enjoy her last chance to demonstrate the lustre of the image claimed for her as the greatest racing schooner of all time!

PROBABLY FEW OF THE MANY who watched the two schooners as they stood at the Boston starting line, on October 9, 1938, realized what they were witnessing: the very last Series of International Schooner Races. If there *was* such an awareness at all, there was no apparent effort on anyone's part to try and parlay it into a spirit of good sportsmanship, which might conceivably lead to future contests. The Series began in a loaded atmosphere. It ended amid recrimination from both sides.

The form of the Series had been changed. The Race Committee, unbalanced by heavy American representation, had decided that three wins would be required of a schooner in lieu of the usual two. So five races were scheduled.

"I told them they could make the Series seven races if they wanted to," Angus said later, "but if they couldn't beat the *Bluenose* in three races, I didn't see as how they expected to do it in five."

For his part, Angus declared he shrank from the possibility of defeat far less than he dreaded the endless daily arguments he was obliged to face. To him, they seemed to be coming from every possible quarter. On the other hand, the Americans loudly claimed *they* were being brought low, not through any superior sailing by *Bluenose*, nearly so much as by the rulings of their own Captain Charlie Lyons, who was Chairman of the Racing Committee. They complained he had sent them out to race when the wind was lacking and held them at dock when it was more than sufficient. Angus countered that he never wanted to race again in American

waters. Only if *Thebaud* cared to sail down to Halifax, in challenge, would she be sure she would find *Bluenose* waiting for her.

There was no blaming the Lunenburg fisherman for his bitterness. His own associates had refused him the money needed to put his vessel into racing trim and take her to Boston. Gloucester authorities then stepped in and guaranteed him $8,000 in expenses, half of which would be delivered in advance. The advance was not forthcoming, and the protest Angus made upon arrival in New England brought a mere $2,000. By the end of the series, $9,000 was owing him, including prize money. It was several months before he managed, with the help of lawyers, to collect $4,300 in settlement.

Neither was he to have the satisfaction of receiving the trophy at the official banquet following the last race of the Series. The cup, he was told calmly, had disappeared. Not until his victory banquet was over was he given the trophy. It was handed to him wrapped in newspapers.

After two races had been sailed, the Americans decided to protest the lengthened water line of the Canadian defender. It was remeasured under supervision by designer Bill Roue, and sure enough, it was two feet longer than the 112 feet specified in the original design. Since there was only one way to rectify matters, five tons of tanks and a lighting plant were removed. Ironically, the change, once made, boomeranged; the old Canadian sovereign of the seas skitted around like a young ballerina.

Neither boat was a spring chicken any longer. *Thebaud* was now eight years old; *Bluenose* was coming up to her eighteenth birthday. Remarkably, she showed no sign of her years, the way she handled.

In the opening tilt of October 9, *Thebaud* established better than a three-minute lead at the outset, lost some of it as she scurried on to the twenty-four-mile mark, then regained a portion to sail over the finish line two minutes, fifty-six seconds ahead. Midway in the fray, *Bluenose* had her foretopmast carried away and so was therefore denied the use of her jib topsail and foretopsail—but the race was really over before that happened. Angus took the beating —for such it was—in good spirit. His sole comment was that only one boat could win and his opponent had sailed a fine race.

Bluenose disdained the usual show of seafaring superstition about the date for the second race, October 13, as she beat the challenger across the starting line. In the thresh to windward, she bettered her lead to over twelve minutes. Following *Thebaud's* example in the opening heat, she lost some of it, but she was never headed, and before the finish re-established it to romp home a good dozen minutes in front of her rival.

Four days later, when she presented herself at the starting line, she was obviously handling sprightlier than ever. Following *Thebaud* over the line, she quickly overhauled the American boat to be four minutes, twenty seconds in the van at the half-way mark. Once again she refused to be headed and swelled the lead to breeze across the finish, six minutes, thirty-nine seconds the victor.

October 24, with the wind varying from eight to twenty-five knots, *Thebaud* evened the score. It was a bitter pill for the Lunenburgers to swallow. *Bluenose* was well out in front when her backstay suddenly let go. Her two masthead men were seriously endangered by the manoeuvre necessary to bring her into the wind so her jib tops'l could be doused. This all took time—too much time—and although her crew worked frantically, she stood no chance of making up the loss. *Thebaud* finished, according to her own crew's timing—for the Committee boat had gone astray in the low visibility that attended most of the race—a good five minutes ahead of the Champion.

Angus swallowed the disappointment.

"*Thebaud* beat us," he acknowledged ruefully as he stepped ashore, "but tomorrow's another day, don't forget!"

Indeed it was. On October 26, 1938—a day few Canadians will ever forget, the *Bluenose* scudded out for her last challenge and defense of her title of Queen of the Seas. As she settled herself to the fifth and deciding race, high, taut canvas canting a curtsy to salt water, as offering a last salute, as though she knew there would be no more calls to battle, no more chances to add further to already unprecedented sailing honors.

The win she forged was by a scant two minutes, fifty seconds, but a win it was . . . decisive, final! On the last leg, her topsail halyard-block gave up the ghost. Otherwise, her ultimate victory would surely have been somewhat more spectacular. Nevertheless, she took it, not in the way of the tired old campaigner she was, but going like a house afire.

Surging toward the finish line, the magnificent Lunenburger stood under way amid a silence as spontaneous as the tumultuous ovation that suddenly burst forth in unrestrained salute to the greatest schooner of them all. The greeting echoed back and forth across the bay. It could not have been more resounding had it issued from the realm of her own home waters. Americans, for all their erstwhile sweat and tears, knew a *champion* when they saw one; they could not, would not, begrudge her one whit due in this moment of supreme triumph.

And so it was that the lovely hull which had slid with such prophetic grace down the ways into the waters of Lunenburg Harbour, nearly eighteen years before, came like a lady to the manner born, to the end of her tournament of glory. She had regained the International Trophy for Canada at first try, and never had she let it go! She had demonstrated an almost fantastic superiority on every single point of sailing, in every kind of weather, light or heavy, and not one of the fine ships that offered threat to her title had prevailed over her.

At the end, whether they had been among those who had striven to dislodge her from her throne, or among the host of others who always had known it couldn't be done, none could any longer disagree with the claim of her indomitable little skipper:

"The wood of the vessel that will beat the *Bluenose* is still growing!"

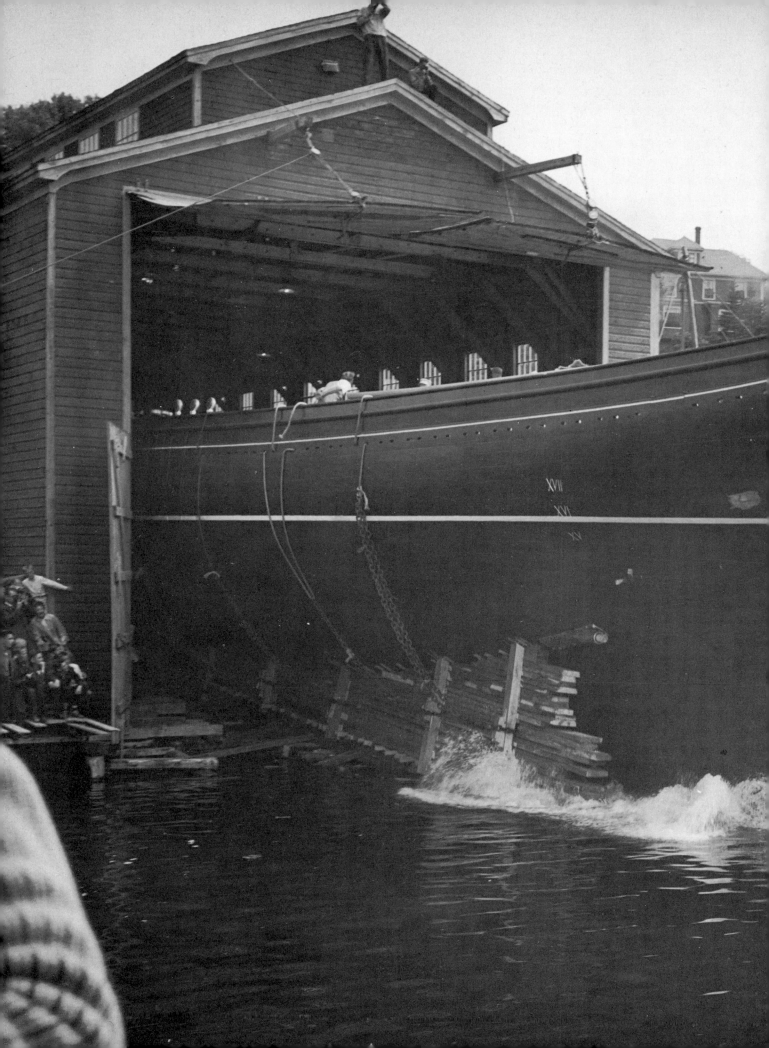

STEPPING A LEGEND

S OON AFTER DAYLIGHT they had started, spotty and quickly at first, then at slower pace as traffic thickened to a steady stream. Before long the highways looked like huge conveyer belts, converging at points of entry; the cars turning off to crawl along to the parking lots or inch into spaces on dozens of side streets, bumper to bumper.

There were thousands of them; like the boats of every kind and description already gathered in the harbour, they were loaded to the gunn'ls. Obviously, folks expected this to be a day of all days and the press and jam was part of the fun. If your windshield sported a sticker marking you as one of four thousand invited guests, you were directed by one of several specially-recruited traffic officers to a pre-arranged parking area. Here, you disembarked with your passengers to board one of a dozen buses providing a shuttle service to the centre of activities. Otherwise, you simply joined the flow of people afoot, moving to the east end of town where the shipyard lay between the shore and the hill rising from it, making a natural amphitheatre of the site.

A quick survey disclosed that the best places of vantage were rapidly filling on a first come basis, whether you carried an invitation or not. You hurried to your choice of a pile of yard-lumber, a roof-top or one of the wharves or marine slips. If you preferred the deck of a craft moored alongside a jetty, there were plenty of these—and of room in the backyards that stretched around the harbour's edge to either side of the shipyard. When you turned to look up the hillsides, behind the temporary grandstand long since packed with invitees, you saw they were blossoming with people.

But wherever you stood, sat or balanced precariously, you came to gaze finally in fascination at the front of a big red shed. Through the opening loomed the forward end of a sleek, black hull, merging a short way back with the darkness of the building's interior. On your way through the yard, if you had passed in front of the hangar-like doorway, you couldn't resist pausing to try and pierce the shadows to the narrow black plank curving along the ship's gunwale, some ten feet above your head. And there you spied the carved and gilded characters that spelled out the storied name: *Bluenose!*

Only, something new had been added . . . the Roman numeral "II"—gleaming as brightly as the letters that preceded it. Then, if you happened to be one of those whose wishes had hastened this day, perhaps even one who had helped bring it to pass (and there were many)—then, and only then, you were wholly willing to believe that a dream was about to come true.

For, in a few short minutes, there would emerge from the shed, the only *fitting* memorial to Canada's long-lost, famous schooner *Bluenose*, —an exact and faithful copy of the great sailing vessel. Here was the *Bluenose* Legend, ever so persistently refusing to die—about to take a new lease on life; impossibly reincarnated!

The bands reached the end of their march to the yard. The last bus delivered its load, three minutes before deadline. Through the loud-speaker system, beamed to hills and harbour, came the words of the opening speeches. And soon, as the printed program in your hand noted, there began the presentation of medallions, specially struck by order of the ship's owners to mark this unusual event.

The Lieutenant-Governor, H. P. MacKeen, congratulated the builders, the sponsors—and, with a special note of meaning, the town—citing its good fortune for what was taking place that day. He said it would be his pleasure to deliver the second medallion to the Governor-General of Canada. There was one also for the Premier of Nova Scotia, Hon. Robert L. Stanfield, unable to be present, but accepted for him by the Province's Minister of Trade and Industry,

Hon. E. A. Manson, who received one for himself as well.

Heads of Governments in the other Atlantic Provinces came in for their share of the striking souvenirs bearing an engraved image of the *Bluenose* and her replica and the date of the latter's launching. The Mayor of Lunenburg, Dr. R. G. A. Wood, also received one; so did the brother-builders of *Bluenose II*, John and Fred Rhuland, whose father had been George Rhuland of the Yard's founding partners; and Rear Admiral Hugh F. Pullen, lately retired from the Royal Canadian Navy, and present as Commodore of the Nova Scotia Schooner Association.

Up to this point, the medals had been presented principally as mementos of the day, as everyone was well aware. Not so the next three, each of which bore an individual and historic significance. The first was handed to Audrey Smith. As a young girl and daughter of the Yard's co-founder, the late Richard Smith, she enjoyed the distinction of having christened the *Bluenose*, that Spring of 1921. The crowd chuckled in approval as she received a hearty buss from Colonel Sidney Oland, Chairman of the firm that had financed the schooner's construction, when he placed the medal in her hands. Next came none other than W. J. Roue, the noted designer of *Bluenose*, now in his eighties and glad, as everyone was for him, to be on hand to see her replica come to life.

There was wide applause as Bill Roue rose to accept his medal . . . a murmur as he begged to be excused from making a speech. The celebrated creator of *Bluenose* was never "much for words," as he had a habit of pointing out, and the crowd knew and understood. A moment later it erupted into cheers as Captain Angus Walters, famed master of the great sailing champion, was beckoned forward to be honoured. The old skipper glowed as the medal came into his hands. To no one else present could the day hold nearly the significance—or half the thrill!

But, in common with all who watched, he found himself hard put to control his emotions when a further gesture of honour was added. Colonel Oland held an illuminated certificate, striking in appearance and lavish in praise of the grand old sea-captain, for whom it had been specially created. About to pass it over, the Colonel hesitated for an instant's reflection; "I'm going to read this to you," he avowed to the delight of the crowd, and did:

Lunenburg — July 24, 1963; Colonel Sidney Oland, whose firm owns BLUENOSE II, presents a commemorative certificate to Honorary Captain Angus Walters prior to the launching of the replica of his famous command.

"Presented to Captain Angus Walters on the occasion of the launching of the schooner Bluenose II, replica-memorial of the original Bluenose, in token of his appointment and acceptance of the post of Honorary Captain of the Ship, and in recognition of the special and lasting place which the immortal Bluenose, undefeated and International Sailing Champion and Queen of the Seas, carved for herself in the hearts of Canadians through her exploits and triumphs under the hand of her Master-Mariner."

Captain Angus stood and savoured the moment to the full as the applause of the crowds echoed around him.

"This," he said quietly, "is the thrill of a lifetime!"

Then, being assured he was indeed welcome to say a few words, he went on to make the best speech of the day!

As he took his seat, not a person present failed to join the salute of cheers that exploded again for the man who was as much a part of the *Bluenose* story as the ship herself.

Among other medals earlier presented was one to Janet Hirtle, the Nova Scotia Fisheries Exhibition's 1962 Queen of the Sea . . . whom Colonel Oland first cited as "one anybody would like to kiss," then promptly demonstrated that "anybody" included himself.

Now, with the big moment but minutes away, the dark-haired beauty walked across the platform with a bouquet of roses for Mrs. Sidney Oland, who would christen the schooner.

Captain Ellsworth T. Coggins,
formerly master of the replica
BOUNTY, commands
BLUENOSE II.

(above) — For more than three hours
a steady stream of cars flows into town
bringing thousands of visitors and guests
to celebrate the return of the BLUENOSE.

(below) — Well aided and abetted, old-time skipper Angus Walters
relishes a rare moment as he balances for a mighty swing to drive a golden spike home
in the keel of his famed charge's replica. Behind him stand (left to right) Victor Oland,
builder Fred Rhuland, designer W. J. Roue
and head of the House of Oland, Colonel Sidney C. Oland.

The chaplains finished the blessing of the ship and a hush fell upon the crowd. Mrs. Oland moved to a spot near the bow, raising high the be-ribboned and traditional bottle of champagne.

"May God bless and protect this ship and all who sail in her. I christen thee *Bluenose II*."

As champagne cascaded over bow and christener alike, the old-time order rang through the air:

"Wedge up!"

There followed the deafening din of clanging mauls, the like of which had not been heard in Lunenburg in many a day. The clamour halted momentarily, then began again, rising to crescendo just before the final order sang out to the men at keel-side:

"Knock down dogs!"

Barely perceptible, a shudder ran through the ship. Then, ever so slowly and smoothly, the great hull began to move. The bow receded from one end of the shed; the stern moved through the other. Quickly the ship gathered way. As rudder met water, the stern dipped deeply, making a curtsy in obeisance to the natural element about to receive and embrace the ship. Inside the shed, her bow rose higher and higher, almost kissing the last rafters farewell, before plunging in a mighty swoop to the depths of full-tide. The whole, lovely sweep of *Bluenose II's* sleek hull became water-borne and glided into the stream.

There has always been something about the launching of a wooden ship that causes a throat blockage in the most hardened landlubber. And, if within you there glimmers more than a spark of love for ships and the sea, you are likely to find yourself transformed. So it was that July morning—ten-thousand-fold—when *Bluenose II* descended to the waiting waters.

Because *this* one was different! To most who watched, this one was like no other launching that had ever happened anywhere in the world before. The roar of welcome that greeted it, the blaring horns and whistles of harbour-craft, the frenzy of hailing voices echoed up and down the bay—deafening, tumultuous! Even the normally unperturbed harbour gulls were startled into senseless, frantic flight. Forever after, the shriek of an occasional Navy jet above the bay in practice flight would seem tame!

It was a soul-satisfying moment of climax. People crowded down the hill to watch the schooner taken in tow; in fine fettle for the next event on the program, they began to stream from the yard. Buses were waiting to transport more than three thousand guests to Lunenburg's Community Centre—site of the Nova Scotia Fisheries Exhibition—for the day's final flourish. Here, Oland's had laid on a party of all parties to top off the celebrations.

The crowds jammed into the main hall and overflowed into the neighbouring Curling Rink. In the former, an unbroken line of tables marched up the center of the floor, groaning under a load of food, highlighted by every kind of fish delicacy imaginable. Other festive boards along the room's sides were set up as temporary bars, for those who preferred the sterner form of refreshment.

At the main door, a late-arriving seaman hailed a fellow-guest whose hand clutched mute but strong evidence of his having been inside.

"Hey," boomed the newcomer, "where can a feller get a drink, seein' as how you know?"

The reply was enthusiastic. "Only go in, man . . . name o' God, I never seen the like! They got it in there by the t'underin' dory-load!"

And so they had! In each of the four corners rested a traditional saltbanker dory, lined with a plastic sheet and loaded to the gunn'ls with chipped ice. Nestled in these were fifteen hundred dozen pints of chilled beer—notably the "Schooner" brand, with a *Bluenose* sailing across its label.

At the rear of the hall, guests filed through the cafeteria-style kitchen where the Ladies Auxiliary of the Fishermen's Memorial Hospital helped Lunenburg's famed sea-chef, Guy Tanner, dispense over two hundred gallons of his lauded fish chowder . . . a brew to gladden the heart of the most exacting gourmet!

On stage, a men's chorus of Oland employees chanted sea ballads and young Michael Stanbury and his "Townsmen" again and again heeded demands for yet another rendition of his specially written new sea chantey, *"The Bluenose Is Sailing Once Again!"* Then, glass or chowder in hand, everyone watched as a small company of former seamen were brought to the stage to be honoured. These were crewmen of the original *Bluenose*, brimming over with reminiscence and the pleasure of renewing long-past shipboard friendships.

On the floor of the auditorium, the refreshments flowed and disappeared, the temperature soared, the clamour of spirited conversation rose to a deafening pitch, and opinion

Colonel Sidney Oland's three sons joined him in quartet dedicated to the rebuilding of the BLUENOSE. Don J. Oland (left, above) administrates her maintenance and scheduling. Bruce Oland (center) R.C.N.R., sailed aboard BLUENOSE II on her hurricane-tossed maiden voyage.
Victor DeB. Oland (opposite top), many-year owner of a Tancook schooner, the ADARE, is a sponsor and skipper of the Nova Scotia Schooner Association.

On Launching day, Michael Stanbury, young Maritime musician and composer, plays his new ballad "The BLUENOSE Is Sailing Once Again"! He was already well known for his "Nova Scotia Song."

Lunenburg natives hosted plenty of visitors (opposite and below) crowding every point of vantage in the town, to help celebrate an event few thought would ever happen. Seats were built in the shipyard for a limited number of guests, in front of the shed which housed the ready-to-launch schooner — but it was first come, first served!

*Colonel and Mrs. Sidney Oland
pose informally for a family camera.*

*An old print, recently rediscovered, shows original BLUENOSE rising on the ways,
sturdy frames naked to timber-setting winter frosts, with outside planking barely begun.*

reached the triumph of loud and unanimous agreement that this had indeed been a day of all days. It was a wing-ding of a party—one thoroughly befitting the occasion; not likely to be soon forgotten, much less ever surpassed!

If you were one of the participants in events on that memorable day, you were probably a willing part of the mass delight. If so, you will neither require nor wish for any analysis of it. But perhaps you were not so fortunate. And if, reading of it now, you become fascinated by the wonder in such a display of affection toward a ship—even a "ship with a soul"—or by such celebration at her return-in-image, then you have to go back a way and pick up the story earlier. Back to where the idea to rebuild the *Bluenose* first began to take form, then assumed more tangible outlines, and finally caught fire, as a way was found at last to bring to pass what more and more people had come to desire so ardently.

FOR A LONG TIME, if anyone had seriously thought of building another *Bluenose* little was heard of it. For years after her loss on a Caribbean reef, Lunenburgers and others indulged in an orgy of self-recrimination over the short-sightedness that had allowed her to meet oblivion. But that was all. Any thought of what else to do about it was yet to be voiced.

It was just after the mid-fifties that to Halifax businessman Victor Oland occurred an interesting idea. It had nothing to do with the *Bluenose*, as such, but it did involve the type of vessel of which she had been the finest example. Oland's thought was to build a full-sized schooner as a publicity vehicle to advertise one of his brewing firm's products with that appellation for a brand name. He had the strong feeling that such a vessel—or better still, *two* of them—would attract wide attention when pitted against each other in privately-sponsored competition. A second result, he figured, was almost bound to be a general spurring of interest in schooner sailing, of which all members of the Oland family, (especially Victor, owner of an ancient but lively Tancook Schooner named *Adair*) were ardent devotees. A third was the bare possibility that the days of international schooner racing might even be revived.

The last was the thinnest kind of hope, for more than the boats were lacking. The changes wrought in the fishing industry over the years would make it next to impossible to find a sufficient number of men for crewing even a single ship. As the trawlers grew in numbers, the old saltbankers disappeared at a rapid rate. So did the schoonermen, who thus lost the only means of honing their sailing skills to the fine edge that would always be necessary for international competition.

In any case, it happened that the brewing firm fell victim to a prolonged strike. All thought of the project had to be laid aside, at least temporarily. By the time consideration of the idea could be renewed, an event took place which changed the whole concept of what Victor Oland had in mind: the building of the movie ship *Bounty* was undertaken at the Smith and Rhuland yard in Lunenburg. This was a development that set the Oland executives and a great many other people to thinking along lines previously unexplored.

The launching of *Bounty* provided a thrill for Lunenburg citizens and visitors alike that led to a wish for more of the same. The commonly-expressed exclamation of the day, that "it might have been the *Bluenose*!" was practically automatic. But it was born of something more than a mere burst of emotion at the sight of an old-time ship's launching. It was inspired as well by the hard-headed business realization that a replica of a storied ship held as great an attraction as the original herself— and a vastly more practical one, when one noted the tremendous interest sparked by the building phase!

Proof of this lay in the stream of pilgrims that, for the several months of *Bounty's* construction, had transformed the south shore town into a daily Mecca for tourists. People swarmed like bees into the hive of fascinating activities, where the traditional, skilled shipwright—admittedly a figure not long for this world—was providing an intriguing observance of age-old crafts and almost-forgotten tools, now so rarely

but still cunningly plied in the ship-building trade.

And so it was that the latent wish to do *something* about the loss of the *Bluenose* became father to the seemingly practical thought of how to re-claim her. True: the magnificent old ship was gone, never to return—but this fact, however sombre, was apparently not unalterable. What more fitting memorial to her greatness than to undertake the building of her replica, whose operation, like that of her predecessor, could—although in a different way—render substantial benefits to her home port and province. As a tourist attraction, she probably would be without peer. In an additional dual-role as hostship to visitors, and far-ranging promotional-vehicle and goodwill ambassador, her potential might well be enormous.

The news that Lunenburg was rife with rumours of building a *Bluenose* replica seemed to fire imagination across the nation. Almost immediately, letters began to arrive from far and near. Addressed to Angus Walters, they enclosed enthusiastic endorsement in the form of cash as well as good wishes. In short order, a movement began to crystallize within the town to build another *Bluenose* by public subscription.

Even those who were keenest for it admitted such a project would not be easy, but they felt strongly that careful planning and determined action stood a good chance of succeeding. They agreed too with a general feeling that building the boat would likely prove to be the easier part of the scheme to achieve. What constituted a far knottier problem was the question of whether operation of such a vessel, in the roles planned for her, would make her self-supporting. From the start it was realized that this was the major consideration. Unless substantial assurance could be had on this point—a reasonable guarantee the ship would not some day become a white elephant—the whole idea had better be allowed to die at the beginning.

There was only one course to chart. At a community meeting called by the Mayor and attended by some three hundred citizens, it was decided at least to proceed with an organized and careful appraisal of the proposal. Steering and sub-committees were appointed to examine capital construction costs, an appeal for funds, operation and maintenance, exploitation and earning potential; these were only some of the points calling for searching investigation and assessment.

The reports most committees made to a

second general meeting a month later were favourable. At one point, the project stood within a hair's breadth of going ahead, but an impasse developed when Captain Walters suddenly decided too much money would have to be sought—even though he was later to reverse this opinion and recognize the financial-affairs committee had merely been realistic in setting a figure of $300,000 as necessary to cover all contingencies. Unavoidably, the disagreement shattered the momentum that had been gained. The scheme ground to a halt.

As matters languished in indecision, even those with the greatest zeal grew increasingly doubtful that the vessel would be able to earn her keep. The longer they reflected, the more loathe they became to commit either themselves or the town to the unknown hazards which the future might present.

By now Captain Angus had had second thoughts and was trying to get things rolling again. Alas, the damage had been done; although he was joined by a small group of loyal supporters, enthusiasm was not to be whipped up a second time. Finally, the group engaged a professional organization to conduct a survey and determine what the chances were for building a replica of *Bluenose* by public subscription, as well as chances for operating her profitably in the future. The answer was gloomy.

Clearly all was lost, unless one last remaining hope could be realized . . . that of finding a commercial concern with private reasons for assuming costs of the entire undertaking. It *was* a hope, but only that. Obviously such a sponsor ought to be one who could both afford, and be willing, to operate the projected ship for the public benefit as well as a private one. Those who were aware of the Oland organization's previous interest in building a schooner of the *Bluenose*-type, now recalled that Victor Oland had shown real interest in a suggestion by Captain Walters, some time before.

They decided the time had come for a new approach to be made to the brewing firm. They could hardly have chosen a better moment for it.

As it happened, the company had been on the point of reviving its plans for an *Oland's Schooner* at the same time Lunenburg's scheme first erupted. In fact, an agreement had already

THE PRESIDENT AND DIRECTORS OF
OLAND & SON LIMITED
REQUEST THE PLEASURE OF THE COMPANY OF

_____

AT THE LAUNCHING OF THE SCHOONER

Bluenose II

ON WEDNESDAY, THE TWENTY-FOURTH OF JULY, 1963, AT 10:45 A.M.
FROM THE SHIPYARDS OF
SMITH & RHULAND LIMITED
LUNENBURG, NOVA SCOTIA

RSVP
"Bluenose II",
Keith Hall, 05 Hollis Street,
Halifax, Nova Scotia

And afterwards at a Reception and Buffet Luncheon
at the Lunenburg Community Center

been concluded with designer W. J. Roue for purchase of the original *Bluenose* plans, the copyright of which Roue had only recently taken care to renew. Then, on hearing of the unexpected developments in Lunenburg, Oland's once again deferred their own proceedings to await results. They felt they could not regard the community's idea as anything but exciting and worthy of support. Not only were they prepared to make a substantial contribution to it, but they felt that a move by them to build a schooner off the *Bluenose's* lines was almost bound to rob the south-shore town's venture of some of its novelty and appeal.

Although their desire to build had sharpened considerably since their initial thoughts in that direction, they continued to hold off—not only while events in Lunenburg ran their full gauntlet, but as long as there seemed to be any hope that Captain Angus could succeed in his own dream. Waiting was not an easy thing to do. The Oland business stature hadn't been achieved without application of good business principles and its executives knew an unprecedented publicity opportunity when they saw one.

So it was that when they were approached by a third party who had been asked to arrange a meeting between them and Angus Walters' committee, they needed little persuasion. Nor was any sales talk required. It didn't take long for all concerned to recognize that for Oland's to assume the role of sponsor offered the most benefit for everyone.

The brewing firm would secure a promotional vehicle of impressive potential, fully due in view of the substantial investment. At the same time, the stringent regulations governing brewery advertising in Nova Scotia would make it impossible for Oland's to benefit in the normal and direct way available to other businesses. However, the firm expected the deleterious effects of the Provincial Liquor Board's Advertising Code to be more than offset by the good that would likely accrue to its corporate image, as the ship played that part of her role which would render her a super tourist attraction of the Maritimes.

As for the town of Lunenburg, it stood to gain all the good offered by the rebuilding of its famous schooner and none of the possible bad. The hazard of the vessel becoming a charge on the town at some future date was completely removed, yet her potential for community benefits was not lessened one whit. After all, it was recognized that if the ship *could* be built

by public subscription, her operation would always have to be charted in whatever areas offered the best chances for monetary returns. More often than not, this was likely to be in waters other than those of Lunenburg Harbour.

True, the administration of her schedule and availability would now be assumed by Oland's, but so would the costs! What's more, the brewing firm offered other assurances of a welcome nature. Victor Oland made these a matter of record when he journeyed to Lunenburg to address the local Board of Trade. For a start, he said his company would feel both honoured and privileged to be entrusted with the task of recreating the *Bluenose*. Almost incidentally he branded as unthinkable the idea of calling for tenders on the job . . . the ship could be built in no other place than the yard that had produced the famous original; any other thought was tantamount to absurdity.

Like the first, the new *Bluenose* would be registered in Lunenburg, would be maintained and refitted there whenever necessary. Her owners also would endeavor to see she spent as much of her time in her home port as economy would allow—an intention Lunenburgers themselves as builders could not have bettered.

But more than that, Victor Oland promised that every year when the time for the Nova Scotia Fisheries Exhibition rolled around, the new *Bluenose* would be in attendance. During the full week of the annual Lunenburg Show, she would be placed entirely at the disposal of the Fair's management; to be used in any way they saw fit, with all proceeds from her operations for that week going to the treasury of the Exhibition.

As to her regular movements and administration, Oland announced the vessel would be used and handled at all times in a manner commensurate with the dignity and bearing of her grand old predecessor. He added his opinion that the new ship should never be raced. As a memorial to the great schooner who had won such a shining record, her existence would become a sorry fact indeed should she ever tarnish the lustre of her progenitor as an unbeatable champion. And finally, in answer to those rumoured to believe that as an Oland vessel she would exist primarily as a freighter of beer, Victor Oland pointed out that a more expensive manner of transporting his firm's products could hardly be devised.

More than one Lunenburg citizen was heard

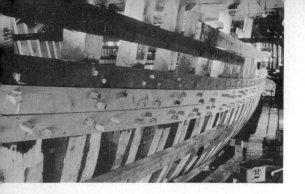

to remark at the Board's dinner that night, "How lucky can we get!"

Before construction could begin, one last element was forthcoming. Captain Lawrence Allen, who had been Angus Walters' mate on the first *Bluenose*, had secured the official rights to the name *Bluenose II*, to grace a sailing miniature he was busily building in his boat shop. He sent word to the Oland firm that on the day they laid the keel for the full-size duplicate of the ship he had known and loved so well, he would present them with the name. He would use another for his own baby *Bluenose*. That did it! The whole project was "off to the races."

THE LAUNCHING OF A WOODEN SHIP is a sight sure to quicken the pulse and enchant the eye. So is the building! The skill evoked in the "working" of various woods; the use of tools, now almost—but not quite—forgotten; the craftsmanship of men tutored by their fathers and the experience of many years in the trade—all these beguile even one who would ply a pen-knife in deadly peril.

Bluenose II, like any other vessel, wood or steel, had her beginning in the laying of a keel, February 27, 1963. If you were among the small company invited to be present on that occasion, you entered the large Smith and Rhuland shed in anticipation of a thrill. You were not disappointed. The great keel lay centered between the ways, running from the building's water-end forward to where the big doors would open back, some five months later, to reveal the bow of a finished hull. As you sighted along the straight line of the fifty-foot keel block, your eye travelled on and up the bow-stem. The whole unit had been painted by the workmen in an orange-red that made it look like a shaft of molten iron; from its size you were sure it must be just as heavy as though it *were* composed of metal. But most of all, those clean, winging lines seemed to conjure in your mind's eye the impression that even at that early moment, the stamp of speed and grace had been implanted.

BLUENOSE II presents a handsome picture . . .
light airs help her try set of sails, test running gear and show
her answer to helm, as her Master, Ellsworth Coggins,
one of best known and ablest saltwater skippers afloat, enables her to emulate
her illustrious predecessor in moving under the hand of a noted captain.

Midway along the keel block, a golden spike was set, waiting to be driven home—just like another time, forty-two years before. In retrospect, you couldn't help smiling to yourself at recalling a noble gentlemen and a befuddled aim. You had the feeling that things would go better this time.

Brief, formal speeches were soon over. Colonel Sidney Oland, Chairman of the Board of Oland's stood poised, be-ribboned maul in hand, ready to emulate (but only in part) that illustrious predecessor, the Duke of Devonshire, upon the keel of *Bluenose*, back in 1921. But the Colonel forebore to hurry. Giving the spike a few, careful taps, he passed the maul to Bill Roue, who added a couple of his own. Then the Colonel passed the mallet to Angus Walters, nodding graciously as he spoke.

"Here, Angus. I think you're the one who ought to be doing this!"

At a spry eighty-odd-years, Angus was still no man for half measures. Surprised and pleased by the gesture, he paused an instant to prolong the feeling of exquisite anticipation. Squinting an eye, he sighted the spike and lined up the big hammer; then, swinging it to a hay-maker arc, he brought it crashing down true to the mark! If the moment was touched with a sort of splendour for the old man, it brought a lump to the throat of everyone who knew how he felt. To a chorus of cheers, the gleaming spike sank home; the building of *Bluenose II* was well and truly under way.

JUST AS FORTY YEARS BEFORE, men fell joyfully to the task before them. Only one or two of them had worked on the first *Bluenose* and certainly under vastly changed circumstances. The new ship was to be built indoors rather than in the open like her predecessor; the better to speed the job, free of the caprices of weather. Whether the move proved worthwhile in the long run is doubtful, for in such close quarters, the men laboured under a constant barrage of interruptions and questions from the hordes of visitors that daily poured through the door of the shed.

Nevertheless, if you were one of them, you were courteously received and allowed to roam at will, so long as you accepted the warning that you did so—as on any other construction site—at your own risk. You watched in fascination as each stage of the building process unfolded and found it almost impossible to tear yourself away and give others a chance to see.

It's the frames, or ribs, that give a ship's hull its shape, and massive is the only word properly describing those they fabricated for *Bluenose II*. Each of her frames was made "double," composed of twin ribs, each measuring eight inches through for a total of sixteen inches of bone-hard oak used in the lower sections, birch in the uppers. Previously sawed-out over patterns, or templates transcribed from the drawing board, they showed the amazing cunning employed in working huge, naturally-curved pieces of timber through the great band-saws in the yard shop.

As you watched the first of these being raised into position by block-and-tackle for the section of the ship amidships, you felt your landlubber credulity stretched to the limit. How could a hull composed of sixty-three sets of these tremendous frames, not to mention all the added weight of planking and a hundred other items, not go straight to the bottom—much less, float with such grace of buoyancy, once it hit the water? But such are the floating properties of wood and the wonders of naval architecture, that not only will the ship indeed remain waterborne, but the builders can calculate beforehand exactly to what depth she will settle in her natural element.

Gradually, over a period of weeks, all sixty-three frames were set in position, towering above the keel and flaring out to either side. Each in its turn was held in position with stays, lined up properly in relation to its neighbours, "ribboned out fair" with battens, and "scarfed in." It was the manner of the "scarfing in" and the fastening of frames to keel that provided the next intriguing sight to the observer.

With all frames correctly spaced—twenty-one-inches-on-centre from each other—the keelson, a heavy beam of spruce to run parallel with the keel, was laid above and rested upon them. The keelson next was flanked on either side by an assistant-keelson; each of these in turn, flanked on its outer side by an assistant-assistant-keelson! All of these strangely-named timbers were cut from spruce, which, being a "long" rather than "short" wood (shipwright's jargon for describing the fibre characteristics) gives an extra bending capacity. Having such a nature, they could be warped more readily or drawn down to conform perfectly with the line ascribed by the top of the keel as it runs the length of the hull.

Nothing could be more elementary than the method of fastening the frames to the keel, using the keelson-members as clamps so to

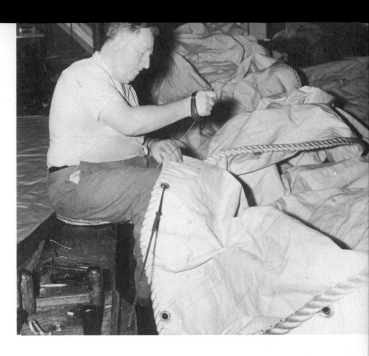

(left) — Fred Rhuland and John Rhuland,
brother builders of BLUENOSE II.
Richard Smith and their father, George Rhuland,
built the original ship.
(above) — Sailmaker Everett Lohnes sews part of
BLUENOSE II's 10,000-square feet of
canvas by hand, as he had the
square sails of BOUNTY only two years before.
(lower left) — Tool of the past —
a caulking hammer in the hands of a yard man,
beats time to the march of oakum along open
seams between heavy deck planking.
(lower right) — A yard hand wields an adze,
ancient tool of the shipwright
serving only practiced hand and eye.

speak, yet the magnitude of the process was amazing to watch. Holes were started through the keelson and its assistants, then bored through the frames and finally down and out through the bottom of the keel itself. Then giant bolts up to six feet in length were threaded through the holes to protrude eventually below the keel's bottom surface. Heavy nuts were fitted on. As the bolts were strained tight, the keelsons were drawn down and bent into the line of the keel, imprisoning the frames in a vice-like grip.

Although the giant-sized bits used to bore the long holes through some six feet of timbers in *Bluenose II* were power-driven, the feat still was not easily or quickly accomplished. One could not help but marvel then at the manpower it must have called for to perform the job in the old days, when the power-drill as we know it now was still a dream.

Still, if you had any doubt that sheer human strength could be equal to the task, you had only to look at the rows of big augers hanging on the walls of the Smith and Rhuland tool-shed. Ranging in length from two to six feet, they

were mute evidence to the proof that the job *could* be done by hand—and was, for hundreds of ships the yard had constructed. So the fact was incontrovertible, and you tormented yourself with another: How was it possible to keep that huge drill headed constantly and precisely at the correct angle? Then you remembered . . . it was such cunning of hand and eye that makes the master shipwright.

With the shape of *Bluenose II* fully framed out to form the rib-cage of the ship, planking was begun. Birch and oak were used for those stretches of the hull below waterline and Douglas fir for the top five "strakes" of freeboard. All planking was secured in the *one* manner providing for the strongest means of fastening known to shipwrights. Instead of metal spikes which draw out under strain, treenails, or "trunn'ls" as they are called, were used. Literally what their name implies, "treenails" are wooden nails, with square heads and unpointed ends to their round shanks. Rendered from hatmatack, they were sledged tightly into holes previously bored through timbers they were to marry together in a

Straight and lipped adzes wielded by veteran shipwrights square a massive length of British Columbia pine as the first step in shaping BLUENOSE II's "sticks."

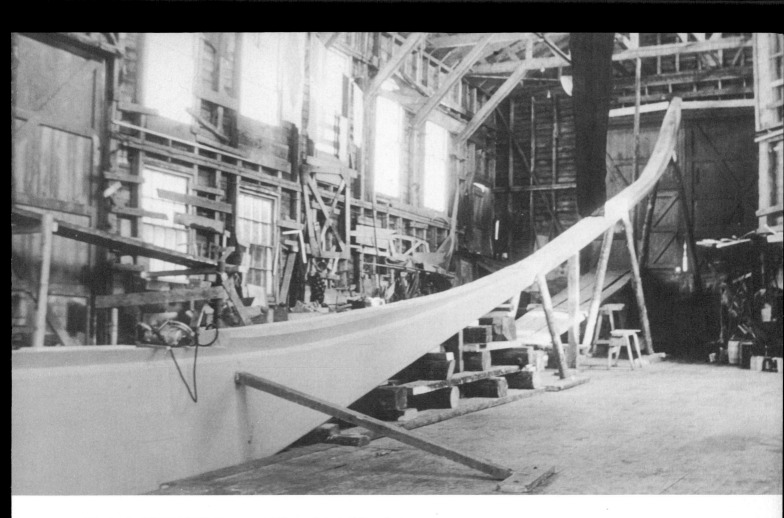

*The keel of BLUENOSE II rests mid-floor of the building shed
awaiting official ceremonies,
to be attended by officials of the Town of Lunenburg and persons having
a connection with the ship's predecessor and a keen interest in her reincarnation.*

union that will never permit divorce on the part of either member. Once fully driven in, the square head and any superfluous end of shank was sheared off, then each end was split open to receive an oak wedge. Thus anchored, they will defy almost any strain made on them to give. Over seventeen thousand of these wooden trunn'ls were used in the construction of *Bluenose II!*

While the planking of the outside was proceeding, a second crew of men took up the job of "ceiling"—the name for planking applied to the *inner* faces of the frames. In this way the ship actually was given a double skin, the inside skin of spruce joining that on the outside in a fabric knitting together keel, keelsons, frames, bow-stem and stern-post to form a mold-like ship's body of terrific strength and rigidity.

Across the gaping maw of this open envelope of wood went solid deck-beams of spruce, coped and fitted to carlings, clamps and shelf strakes to form a heavy gridwork. Upon this, carpenters laid down a deck of stout, clear-pine planks. Then the caulkers moved in. Lately

finished with their work on the ship's sides, their strange-looking caulking-mallets beat a steady tattoo on wide chisels, forcing coarse oakum into the deckseams. In the days of the first *Bluenose*, pitch had always been used to cover the oakum as a final filler, bringing the seams flush to deck-level. All well and good, until a sojourn in southern climes, when the hot sun would bring the gooey mass boiling out and demanding repeated attention.

It would never do for this ship, likely to winter annually in the Caribbean. Something better had to be found—and was, in the miracle world of plastics, to be combined with a specially-developed glue. The result makes for a seam-filler that refrains from hardening absolutely; remains just pliable enough to give as the wooden planks alternately swell or shrink. But it stays totally unaffected by the searing rays of the sun.

As the deck was completed, various-sized openings were either left or sawn out to accommodate housings, cabin house, stanchions or masts, each—except for the last two—built of

BLUENOSE II shows her long, clean sweep of hull as she slides into her launching waters.

mahogany and firmly fitted and fused to the ship by the Lunenburg shipwrights in a manner generally reserved for fine cabinet-making.

But it was as the ship's rails were fashioned out in diamond-hard birch and oak that one enjoyed the chance to observe the consummate skill of the master-craftsman and his pride in a job well done. Shaped out in the rough, then worked to a finish worthy of a table top, their sturdy hardwood lines rode the gunwales as cleanly as the track of a ski on fresh snow. They appeared to have been poured into place rather than wrought from huge logs of crude timber. Only by the closest examination could you discover where one piece ended to flow imperceptibly into the beginning of another.

Now, with basic construction on the hull completed, every inch of surface on the ship's sides and deck underwent hours of steady sand-

ing to that state of utter perfection deemed necessary in preparation for the first, priming, coat of paint. When this had been applied, the sanding began all over again, almost as though it hadn't been done before. On the stretches of freeboard began to appear the enamel-like, midnight glaze of a blue-black finish coat. Down the vessel's sides it flowed, from rail to neat, white stripe separating the hull's dark-hued top from its underbody of rust-red. And thus she stood, finally, in the same familiar colour-scheme sported by her predecessor.

With a trio of last outside touches supplied by her illustrious name-boards at the bow, and the lettering of *Bluenose II* across her stern, she slid from the shed on launching day, the very spit 'n image of her grand forebear in every respect but one . . . she wore no bowsprit.

For a time, her builders had considered

knocking out a hole in the shed's front to allow her "stick" to be set. They quickly thought better of it—and for good reason. Undoubtedly it would have snapped away like matchwood against the building's rafters in the course of launching. As it turned out, even without it, her unadorned bow barely cleared those stout roof-beams as the stern plunged deep into waiting waters. Yet its absence occasioned some regret for many a Lunenburger who had hoped to see her perfectly duplicate the picture of the old ship as *she* had glided out into the self-same stream so many years before.

Losing way under the trailing restraint of pre-launch supports clinging to her sides like nautical after-birth, the new-born beauty soon floated at rest in mid-harbour and was taken in tow for the wharf, there to be completed below deck and rigged above.

CREATING BLUENOSE II as a memorial-replica required that, at least above water, she be as exact a copy of her original as cunning of hand and eye could make her. But such duplication could be applied only to silhouette of hull and rig. As a modern-day carrier of passengers, she was obliged by a number of factors to be as dissimilar to the old vessel below decks as it's possible to imagine.

No member of the original's salty crews, used to the sight of rough bulkhead and rugged quarters, would find even the smallest similarity in the replica's nether regions. For one thing, today's Department of Transport Steamship Regulations dictate that *Bluenose II* conform to a variety of standards totally undemanded of her progenitor. But in addition, the requirements of passenger comfort, together with the splendour of panelled woods and striking decor, would convince a saltbankerman, at first glance, that doubtlessly he had imbibed too freely and had been shanghaied aboard some Yankee Pasha's yacht.

The interior of the first *Bluenose* can be said to have been basically divided into cabin, hold,

Greeted by cheers and bleating horns,
BLUENOSE II starts to swing her bow toward harbour mouth and open sea.

and fo'c's'le. Within the newer edition reigns the finish and effect of a luxury cruise-ship.

Beginning a few feet from the stern rail, a large cabin-house covers the sunken area containing Captain's Cabin with Chartroom, as well as five private staterooms. Complete in every detail, these are panelled in darkly-grained walnut—and fitted with the most modern of sea-going plumbing facilities. Immediately forward of this area is the Engine Room, and beyond that a small cargo hold for ship's stores, spare parts, and sails. Next comes a good-sized Saloon, providing ample room for passengers to relax and enjoy themselves, safe and dry out of the weather.

Beyond the Saloon is the ship's Galley, as fully equipped as the most modern of present-day kitchens with every mechanical aid for the preparation of hot meals. Between Galley and Saloon is a Chef's Pantry, to hasten the serving of food. The fo'c's'le, or crew's quarters, occupying the bow portion of the ship, includes staterooms for the Mate and Engineer.

All of these interior workings were installed as *Bluenose II* lay to the Yard's wharf, and it was this phase of construction alone which it was not possible to allow visitors to witness. Quarters were far too close to permit otherwise; even the occasional, privileged few, being conducted on the odd tour below deck, were no small hindrance to the shipwrights in their rush to complete the ship as early as possible for sea trials.

But if the magnificence of the new schooner's innards would have confounded the saltbanker-man of yesteryear, her equipment and electronic devices, her navigational aids and sailing luxuries, would have left him standing in starry-eyed unbelief! One can well imagine something of that worthy's reaction to a schooner completely equipped for alternate air-conditioning and heating, quite impervious to the whims of weather . . . his astonishment at the miracle of her ship-to-shore Radio Telephone . . . the wonders of a Direction Finder, a Fathometer, Decca Radar and Loran Navigator. All or any of these mechanical brains stand ready and able to take the place of many an oldtime sea captain, famed in legend by the ability to "smell" his position or his way through "t'ick o' fog;" or the envied possession of corns and bunions endowed with a wondrous ability to give fore-warning of a "blow."

Perhaps the schoonerman of forty years ago might not be quite so soundly amazed at

View from BLUENOSE II's mainmast crosstrees showing aft area.

BLUENOSE II with bowsprit and lower masts stepped is towed to outfitter's basin.

View from foremast showing bow and fo'c's'le head area.

Topmasts, booms and stays in place, BLUENOSE II awaits completion of rigging.

Bluenose II's two one hundred seventy-horse-power caterpillar engines, and perhaps not even by her generating plants. Probably though, he would hail with cuss-saving satisfaction her powerful pumps, viewing them as long-overdue improvement. Chances are he would be some-what more than mildly taken with her variable-pitch propellers as he would with her stainless steel shafting, for the fisherman of the twenties was no stranger to the value of good engineering, let alone the wish for better means to power and maintenance. But this much is sure! His hoot of derision at a complete ship's intercommunication system would surely put to shame any blast of an ancient skipper depending on lung-power alone to roar out an order to "shake a leg and set fisherman's staysail!"

Yet when all is said and done, a saltbanker-man suddenly reincarnated from the lusty days of the first *Bluenose* and plunked amid the facts and "fantasies" of her replica, scarcely would be more intrigued than we, watching in turn the practice of skills now almost extinct. More's the wonder, if truth be admitted, that enough practitioners of those ancient arts remained to recreate so faithfully a ship of former days, for the most part, precisely because they used the exact, self-same techniques of *her* own era.

There was a time when the adze, the draw-knife and spokeshave were all common and necessary tools in every shipwright's chest. Today, these and many others are archaic relics of a dying trade. Strange, even weird-looking, implements they are, that make you wonder that anything so crude in appearance could possibly coerce the most stubborn wood into almost any shape and line desired! But see them wielded! In the hands of a Lunenburg master-shipwright, the adze—probably the most un-gainly of all—becomes a chisel in the hand of the sculptor.

Webster describes the "Spokeshave" as a tool "originally used to shape the spokes of a wheel, but generally used for trimming and smoothing rounded surfaces." Yet it at least is what one might label a "logical" tool, seeing that the results it achieves emerge as what reasonably might have been expected. Not so with the adze, which is difficult even to describe. It's probably as apt as anything to say it looks like a cross between a pick-axe and a garden hoe. The head mounts a large, slightly -curved blade, with a cutting edge measuring about five inches in length, honed razor-sharp, and set at right angles to a snakelike handle.

Plied with a chopping action, one is certain it can deliver only rough results.

But in essence, what the able adze-man actually contrives can only be described as "whittling" on the grand scale, though with a finesse and precision that would do credit to a carver of miniatures. Hardly a timber in the great hull and amidst the lofty rigging of *Bluenose II* but felt the march of its assault or yielded to its inexorable edge. And at no point in the ship's construction was its cunning so tellingly demonstrated as when the time arrived for fashioning the mighty spars.

"Shaping out the sticks" they call it in the language of ships, and it was the sight most worth the watching! The rendering of a ninety-foot mast from a huge baulk of timber measuring two-feet-square at the butt, into a perfect dowel, tapered ever so gently toward one end, is some-

thing that must be seen to be believed. Otherwise, no explanation for such a beautiful piece of work would seem plausible but that an entire tree-trunk must surely have been "turned" on a giant's lathe.

Surprisingly, the thickness of a great chunk of Douglas fir, like that required for the main-mast of a 143-foot schooner is no guarantee against its bending out of alignment through sheer force of bulk as it is laid along the ground upon regularly spaced blocks. Before being worked, it *must* lay absolutely straight. Heavy-duty jacks were placed at intervals along one side, between the huge log and a parallel pile of enormous timbers from which, later, were to come another mast, plus all the booms and gaffs. Stationed at the bigger end, foreman Johnny Rhuland bent to squint an experienced eye along its length, then specified by word of

(below) Escorted by a noisy armada of pleasure craft, BLUENOSE II crosses an old finish line and enters Halifax harbour for the first time. Ashore, more than 50,000 people crowd the shore and breakwater to hail her arrival.

mouth and hand exactly where adjustments were to be made. As now here, now there, jacks translated signal to movement, the big timber was forced with many a protesting grunt to inch its way slowly into the ultimate of straight-lined perfection.

One long last look satisfied John Rhuland's keen eye. "Alright boys, I guess that's got her pretty good. Let's go!"

Down each side of the mast-to-be moved a half-dozen men, adzes hewing faultlessly true to the blue lines chalked end to end to chart the way, whirring chips off the two uppermost longitudinal corners. When they "fetched up" at the heavier end, the stick had six sides along its length instead of the original four. Laboriously it was rolled, bringing the remaining square of it up top for the previous process to be repeated along the still right-angled corners, thus completing the transition from square log to octagonal.

The lower, foot-end of the mast was left in this form, ready for more solid stepping later through an opening of similar dimensions, sawed out of the schooner's deck to accommodate it. About ten feet from the opposite, or aloft-tip, a flat face of a couple of feet or so was left to fore and aft of the round, to provide a secure purchase for the crosstrees. But except for these two sections, the rest of the heavy wooden shaft had to undergo further shaping. Gradually but steadily it changed form—first becoming twelve-sided, then sixteen, then a mass of multiple planes, as the rough-round of the final stage came into being.

Then spokeshaves and smoothing planes came into play, shearing roughness to a satin-like finish. When these were through their share in the work, the mainmast was as perfectly round as if it had been delivered out of some giant tubular mold. And so it went for the better part of three weeks, as the foremast—next on schedule—was shaped out; then in turn, the topmasts, the booms, gaffs and bowsprit. Finally, all wooden members of the schooner's rig lay neatly assembled at boat-side.

By now it was September, and a charming old custom known as "setting the sticks" could be followed for the first time in many Lunenburg years. Foremast and mainmast were derricked up to be lowered through the deck openings awaiting them. As each was settled into its step, a small cache of coins was placed beneath, traditionally a sop to the winds of fortune. Included were Canadian Silver Dollars and Ten-Cent pieces—the latter bearing the effigy of *Bluenose*; launch-marking medallions and some rare old Spanish Doubloons and Pieces-of-Eight, having a special significance because of the Oland family's Spanish ancestry.

With both sticks well and truly set, it was time for the riggers to go into action. They swarmed aloft and soon shrouds and stays appeared, pulling the spars into fair position and securing them firmly against the tests to come. Sheets and running gear were left to dangle briefly until the great sails arrived to be bent on. These had been in work for many weeks at the nearby sail-loft where sail-maker Everett Lohnes had laboured away, cutting, stitching and sewing the more than ten thousand feet of heavy white canvas required for the complete "suit."

No rigging or sail-bending job of equal magnitude had been seen in the south shore port for a couple of decades; not until the summer of 1960 when *Bounty*'s squares'ls had bloomed under the same expert hands. Their work on *Bluenose II* drew close attention and fascinated interest from the crowds who watched daily. Each man knew he was engaged in the performance of a swansong of sorts, and was determined to contribute his best toward creation of a final masterpiece.

How well they succeeded and matched the work already wrought by other hands was demonstrated sooner than anyone anticipated. On her maiden voyage in the early part of January, 1964, to the West Indies by way of Bermuda, *Bluenose II* fully emulated the legendary seaworthiness of her great predecessor. Barely a day out of Lunenburg, manned by an admittedly green crew, she ran smack into a roaring hurricane registering winds up to one hundred miles per hour! Aboard by invitation was Angus Walters. There was also a thrilled working-guest in the person of Commodore Ralph L. Hennessy, Royal Canadian Navy, together with Bruce Oland—himself a Commander in Canada's Naval Reserve, and representing the sailing loves and interests of the owning family. Arrived at Bermuda, every man among them, crewman and guest alike, launched into lyrical praise for the ship and her early-proven ability to weather the sort of fury the sea reserves to loose only in its ugliest moods.

From Angus came a tribute not likely to be soon forgotten. "I'll be frank with you, I was worried. In all my years at sea I only remember one blow that might have been worse—at least it was equally as bad—and that was when we brought the *Bluenose* back from England, that trip over there. But this ship stood right up to it. I doubt if we even shipped a lick of green water. She's a fine one, no doubt of that!"

Once the eye of the hurricane was reached, a foresail was reefed smartly and the ship hove to for thirty hours, riding it out. A few weeks later she was to repeat her performance when she ran into similar conditions lashing out of a storm in the Caribbean. "After that," declared her captain, Ellsworth Coggins, "I'd sail her anywhere in the world under any weather!"

Coggins should know, for the man chosen to be first skipper of the new schooner is no stranger to the trials of seamanship. At the tender àge of sixteen, Ellsworth Coggins left home in Weymouth, Nova Scotia, to begin a career on the water. He was only nineteen when the death of his captain at sea thrust him into his first command, but he completed the ship's voyage before returning her to her owners. With some goodly "stints" in sail and steam logged, he joined up to serve in World War II as an Able Seaman in the Naval Reserve, to be released at war's end in 1946 as a Lieutenant. Rejoining in 1949, as a Lieutenant-Commander, he captained in turn an algerine and mine sweepers. Then he sailed the Navy's sloop, *Oriole*, from Halifax to Vancouver by way of the Panama Canal.

Leaving the Navy for good in 1959, he was summoned from retirement some two years later to take over his most glamorous command. Metro-Goldwyn-Mayer wanted him to skipper the *Bounty*, replica of Captain William Bligh's storied, 18th Century full-rigger. Training a new-found crew in the intricacies of square-sail, Coggins took *Bounty* to Tahiti via the Panama, for the filming of the new screen-version of the lusty Nordhoff and Hall epic, "*Mutiny on the Bounty*." Returning the ship from Tahiti to her owners in Los Angeles, he resumed his command of her six months later, to pilot her on a world-wide publicity tour on behalf of the picture. He delivered *Bounty* on schedule to her owners, this time at the Port of New York, in time for the world-premiere of the movie spectacular.

One of the *Bounty's* crewmen has said of his skipper: "The Old Man was sort of image and antithesis to Captain Bligh. Bligh himself could have handled our ship no better . . . yet I never once, in the worst of blows, ever heard the Old Man holler somebody down. He knew the ship as well as he knew us, and we all worked our butts off for him."

Bounty's log records more than a full measure of trials and tribulations at sea and in port. Those of the latter represent the not-inconsiderable hazards to a ship on exhibition, especially one under constant threat of visits by well over a million admiring (and just naturally) souvenir-hunting boarders. But the log bears no instance of serious damage to the ship from any quarter, man or element. By the time the final tour had ended, both the *Bounty* replica and her captain had become world-known in their own right.

It seems especially appropriate for the second *Bluenose* to answer like the first to the hand of a veteran deepwater skipper. Anything less would be unworthy of the destiny that has permitted the stately old saltbanker to be reincarnated in the lovely lines of a full-size, sailing replica of her handsome self.

Back in 1921, the *Bluenose* came from the stocks at a cost of $35,000. Her replica represents a building figure of over a quarter-million. How well *Bluenose II* will justify such a substantial investment, only time and the future can disclose.

Undoubtedly the odds are in her favour. An international awareness, which through the years has continued to be thrilled by the mere tales from the *Bluenose* legend, will doubtless be moved to see and know more intimately the tangible evidence of it. But, however she fares in the crass world of modern tourism and as a promotional vehicle so readily employable to the good of Nova Scotia, her stature as something else, something more, will forever be unassailable. She stands, for all time to come, as a symbol of affection for a ship which surely has no parallel in the history of the sea.

For here, in the year 1963, began a new chapter—an Epilogue, if you will—to the tale of a lowly saltbank fishing schooner, who fastened so tight a hold on the heartstrings of the people she thrilled and glorified, as to move them—a quarter of a century after her passing—to refuse to accept for her that empty, tired old epitaph: "We shall not see her like again!"

Able heir to a famed command,
Capt. Ellsworth Coggins orders jib and foresail up. . .

as the bow of a new BLUENOSE swings slowly
seaward.

With four lowers and two tops'ls set,
BLUENOSE II eases into Atlantic swells.

Capt. Angus Walters, 81-year-old master
of the original BLUENOSE,
eyes her sister aloft and tests her response.

Reminiscent of many an oldtime contest,
at the height of excitement, the wind fails.

"She feels pretty good. . .
but I wish we could have a little gale!"

Builder Fred Rhuland, author Phil Backman,
Skippers Coggins and Walters
take early measure of her qualities.

Wind freshens,
she heels over and takes up a bone in her teeth . . .

as guests and crewmen leap for her lines.

Eager and confident she heads into it,
displaying her sister's spirit.

Racing helmsman Jack Pardy
joins Captain Angus at the wheel.

Seventeen years gone, BLUENOSE sails again.

epílogue

ON A DAY IN NOVEMBER, 1963, the wind blew lightly out of the east'rd, wetted by occasional drizzle. An army of cameramen, reporters and unswerving devotees to an old love had descended on Lunenburg. In the romantic sense, they were there to share in a rare and strange act of remembrance . . . the debut of an extraordinary and permanent reappearance. In the more practical one, they were on hand to record and participate in the first sailing trials of a smart new schooner, fresh from the hands of her builders.

Aboard was a sprinkling of hands from an earlier storied ship's crew, as well as a part complement of the newer one's, still to be filled out. But none of them, whether recalling old thrills or anticipating unfamiliar ones, quite harboured feelings equal to those showing in the gaze of the grand old man at the helm . . . weather-eye cocked aloft, hands clutched in knowing grip on the wheel-spokes of *Bluenose II*. There was the set of other days to his head as he "listened" to the lay of the ship, heeling over under a brief spate of breeze, and the look of him spoke thoughts the rest of us could only imagine.

"Look at Angus," chuckled Don Oland. "If you had a mind to take that wheel from him, I imagine you'd have to break his arm!"

I hadn't the slightest doubt of it, or any intention of putting so obvious a fact to the test. I walked aft toward the wheel-house and sidled up to stand by the old helmsman. Forty years had added somewhat to his weight, but they had taken little toll of alertness from the mind or figure. Whatever time had wrought, it had not dulled the spirit; merely mellowed to a glow the fire that had ever been ready to flame out at anyone daring to suggest his great *Bluenose* could not meet all comers and vanquish the lot. He gentled the wheel, guiding this new image of his beloved in the way she should go and I had trouble making the words come.

"How is she, Angus?"

The greatest competitive sailing skipper of them all nodded slowly, betraying much of what the moment held.

"She'll do fine," he said. "She's a little down by the head . . . just a little, and maybe a trifle sluggish; but that's only a matter of trimming and we'll soon fix that. All in all, she'll do fine!"

But I was remembering another day, another answer; a shorter one and gilded with the inimitable charm of the ancient Lunenburg way of speaking:

"She's a wery good wessel."

MacAskill

LENS LOG of an Era

John Masefield once wrote this finest of all marine photographers to ask a favour. The great fishermen carriers of fore-and-aft sail were going the way of their square-rigged predecessors. Would the craftsman undertake to record the last of the schooners, in detail, so that future model-makers might more accurately reproduce them? Britain's Poet Laureate was asking no mere contribution to nautical history of a fond romantic. MacAskill was the complete master of his subject and his love. There was simply no one else able to render it captive in such unforgettable fashion.

*BLUENOSE heels over, close-hauled and makes up to weather —
another victory in her wake.*

Four views of BLUENOSE's deck gear (from top: port bow, midships, helm, stern). Seen beside a wharf after a fishing trip to the Banks, dirty, strewn with coils of line, fitted with dories and fishing gear and laden with barrels, BLUENOSE belies the canny sweep of sheer and brand of rigging that lent her incredible speed. Note the three interlocked links painted on her stern, symbol of International Order of Oddfellows and a sure mark of a Lunenburg schooner.

On the slip at Lunenburg,
BLUENOSE shows the fast, clean sweep of her winning lines.
During her construction, her freeboard was raised a foot and a half in bow
to afford more fo'c's'le room.
The result, said many, ruined her forward sheer;
but it did not spoil her racing ability and gave her bow the curious hook
that was one of her most distinguishing features.

BLUENOSE, all sails drawing, in a run down the wind . . .
one of MacAskill's best liked views of the great racer.

Riggers scramble to fit a jib, fresh from the sail-loft, as BLUENOSE prepares to meet a new challenger.

(opposite) BLUENOSE running wing and wing in the trough of tumbling swells.

Sun and shadow strike a nostalgic mood on vessels moored along the Halifax waterfront.

(opposite) "Starboard Lookout" — one of MacAskill's best-loved studies.

Becalmed in the path of the sun, schooners
barely make headway as their crews implore a good breeze for a good race.

First elimination race off Halifax, October, 1921.

Reaching before a strong wind,
BLUENOSE leads COLUMBIA on the homeward leg of the course.

*Caught in a dead calm, two nautical gladiators present
a striking study in light and shadow.*

Lunenburg waterfront — circa 1920.

First Elimination Contest — ALCALA follows
on heels of INDEPENDENCE, CANADIA and BLUENOSE (leading),
out front.

(*above*) *THEBAUD leading* BLUENOSE *at race start.*

(*opposite above*) BLUENOSE, *wearing a borrowed, tan fishermen's staysail leads* THEBAUD *over the line at the start.*

(*opposite below*) BLUENOSE, ALCALA *astern and* CANADIA *abeam, stands at starting line.* INDEPENDENCE *glints in sun behind them.*

In the autumn of 1920, the ESPERANTO (below)
handily defeated the Lunenburger DELAWANA and sailed home with
the International Trophy and $4,000.00, to the greatest greeting
ever accorded a Gloucester vessel. It was her last race.
Six months later the schooner struck a Sable Island wreck and sank.

Over the line — "Like all the hounds of hell were after her"
— BLUENOSE wins her last race against COLUMBIA.

*ALCALA overtakes INDEPENDENCE to leeward
as both schooners broad reach on the port tack during the first elimination
series off Halifax, 1921.*

"*Gray Dawn*" — (*opposite*)
MacAskill's famed and sombre study, hung in over 30 International Salons.

A Lunenburg schooner bites into
rolling Atlantic swells during the first elimination race, October, 1921.

Once a common sight in every Atlantic village,
and spawn of the great saltbankers — acres of salt cod curing
in the sun and destined for the markets of the world,
now usurped by steel draggers and trawlers
and their production of quick-frozen fish.

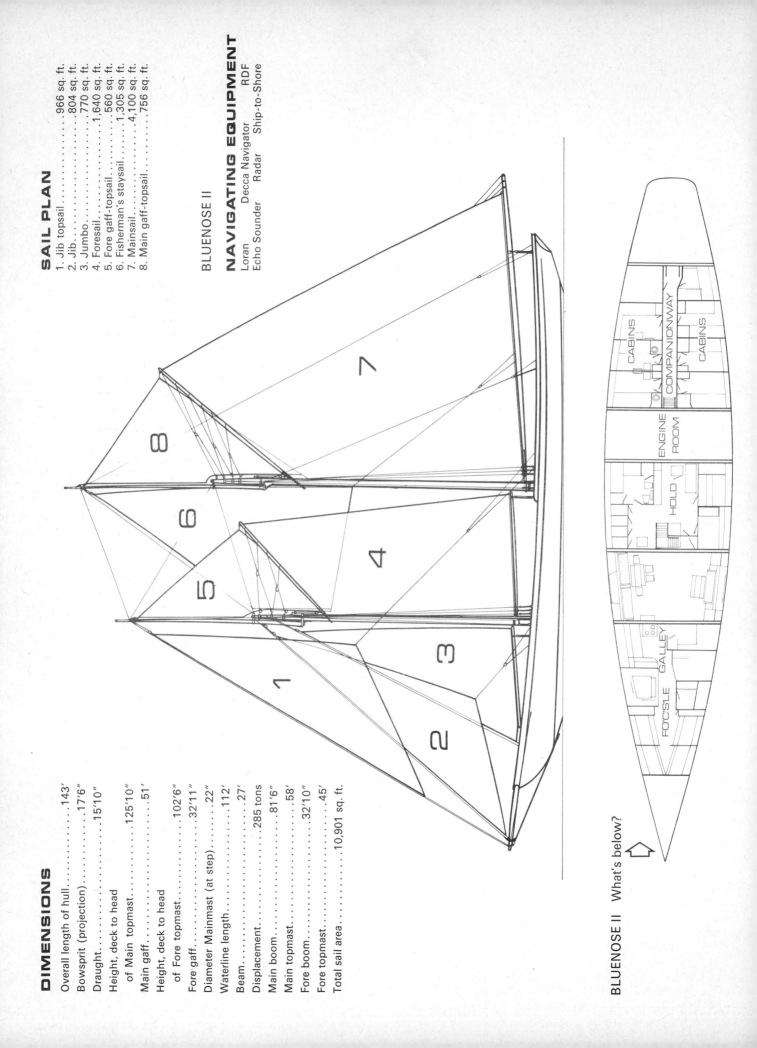

DIMENSIONS

Overall length of hull..............143'
Bowsprit (projection)............17'6"
Draught.............................15'10"
Height, deck to head
　of Main topmast...............125'10"
Main gaff.............................51'
Height, deck to head
　of Fore topmast................102'6"
Fore gaff..............................32'11"
Diameter Mainmast (at step).........22"
Waterline length.................112'
Beam.................................27'
Displacement..................285 tons
Main boom......................81'6"
Main topmast......................58'
Fore boom.......................32'10"
Fore topmast......................45'
Total sail area..........10,901 sq. ft.

SAIL PLAN

1. Jib topsail.................966 sq. ft.
2. Jib............................804 sq. ft.
3. Jumbo........................770 sq. ft.
4. Foresail...................1,640 sq. ft.
5. Fore gaff-topsail..........560 sq. ft.
6. Fisherman's staysail.....1,305 sq. ft.
7. Mainsail..................4,100 sq. ft.
8. Main gaff-topsail.........756 sq. ft.

BLUENOSE II

NAVIGATING EQUIPMENT

Loran　　Decca Navigator　　RDF
Echo Sounder　　Radar　　Ship-to-Shore

BLUENOSE II　What's below?

The gathering of material for this book started some years before actual writing began. Having natural love and pride for the BLUENOSE, we nevertheless were determined to present a fair and factual record of her career, as well as an unbiased account of each series in which she first won and then successfully defended her crown. In cases of contentious rulings by committees, decisions of judges and actions on the part of crews and skippers, every known source of information was carefully explored. To this end many people were interviewed and a large number of records and press stories of the day sifted and correlated. The list of these is too numerous to be set down here, but we are especially grateful to the following:

To Captain Angus Walters for his patient, careful attention to all our inquiries and for his honest and painstaking effort in reading proofs and helping us set the record straight; to Sterling Hayden, Actor and Author of "WANDERER" (Alfred A. Knopf Inc.), whose experiences as a young crewman aboard the GERTRUDE L. THEBAUD provided an invaluable reference; to Eric Hamblin for his helpful criticism and Bruce Law for his tremendous assistance in art; then, to a host of Lunenburgers and former BLUENOSE crewmen; notably builder Fred Rhuland, Captain Lawrence Allen, Mr. Moyle Smith, the late Loren Geldert, Town Clerk of Lunenburg, shipwrights John Rhuland, Dan MacIsaac, Howard Faulkenham, and the late Creighton Zinck, and not least to Solomon Morash, grand old-time shipbuilder and master craftsman, dead these 33 years, but whose superb yarns still come through loud and clear.

In addition, we are obliged to many others whose suggestions, advice and encouragement constitute the kind of assistance that turns much of the labour of writing into work that's a pleasure.

News stories and accounts from The Halifax Herald and The Halifax Chronicle were particularly informative and helpful. These were consulted in depth.

To those wishing to know more of the story of the BLUENOSE: we recommend the reading of Jerry Gilespie's "BLUENOSE SKIPPER" (Brunswick Press), wherein they will find, as we did, so much to interest and enthrall - and also, "SCHOONER BLUENOSE" (Ryerson Press) by the late Andrew Merkel, to whom, for his clear account of the various international sailing contests, we owe special gratitude.

Finally, this book will be a lasting testament to the craftsmanship of Nova Scotia photographers, who together with the great W. R. MacAskill have supplied a magnificent pictorial record of both the BLUENOSE and her replica, BLUENOSE II. Photographic Credits in detail will be found overleaf.

THE AUTHORS

The Canadian Ten-Cent Silver Piece showing BLUENOSE. Minted, January 1, 1937.

The Canadian Fifty-Cent Bluenose Commemorative Stamp. Issued in Blue, January 6, 1929.

PHOTOGRAPHERS' CREDITS

Brian Backman - Pages 10, 22, 27. Phil Backman - Page 20. Cal Productions - Pages 80 and 81 - deck shots. Maurice Crosby - Page 67, Pages 80 and 81 - sailing views. John Holmes - Page 7 - photo of Jack L. Gray painting. PO₂ Eugene Hovey, RCN - Pages 76, 112. John E. Knickle - Page 13. W. R. MacAskill - Pages 9, 10, 11, 16, 17, 24, 25, 27 - bottom, 28, 29, 31, 33, 34, 37, 39, 41, 47, 48, 84; Pages 86 to 109 inclusive. Lee Wamboldt - Page 79. Terry Waterfield - Page 83. Cliff Wright - Pages 52/53, 57, 60 - top right and bottom, 61 - centre and bottom, 64. Charles E. Young - Pages 21, 23, 55, 58 - bottom, 62, 66, 69, 70, 71, 72, 73, 74, 75. Keith Young - Page 69 - two at bottom. Book Cover Photos Front and Back by Maurice Crosby.

Published by McClelland & Stewart Limited. Printed by John Deyell Company. Design and Layout by Phil Backman. Special Art and Design Consultant, Bruce Law. Typographical Advisor - John P. Wright.